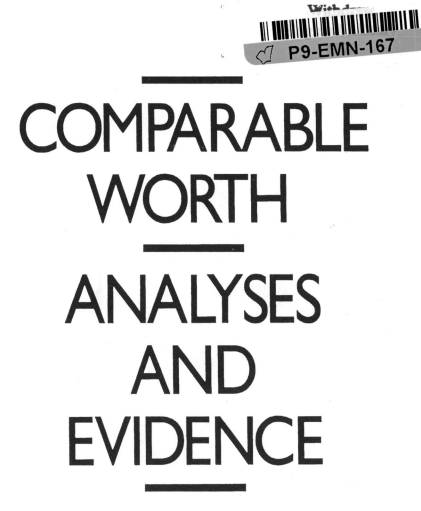

COMPARABLE WORTH

ANALYSES AND EVIDENCE

EDITED BY M. ANNE HILL & MARK R. KILLINGSWORTH

ILR PRESS
New York State School of Industrial and Labor Relations
Cornell University

Cover design: Kat Dalton

Library of Congress Cataloging-in-Publication data

Comparable worth : analyses and evidence / edited by M. Anne Hill and
Mark R. Killingsworth.
   p. cm.
   Papers and comments presented at a colloquium held at Rutgers
University, Oct. 9, 1987.
   Bibliography: p.
   Includes index.
   ISBN 0-87546-147-6.—ISBN 0-87546-148-4 (pbk.)
   1. Pay equity—Congresses. 2. Labor supply—Congresses.
I. Hill, M. Anne. II. Killingsworth, Mark R., 1946–   .
HD6061.C636   1989
331.2'1—dc 19   89-2063
                                                                          CIP

The paper used in this publication meets the minimum requirements of American
National Standard for Information Sciences—Permanence of Paper for Printed
Library Materials, ANSI Z 39.48–1984.   ∞

Copies may be ordered from
ILR Press
New York State School of Industrial and Labor Relations
Cornell University
Ithaca, NY 14851–0952

Printed in the United States of America
5 4 3 2 1

CONTENTS

PREFACE

THIS volume contains papers and discussants' comments that were originally presented at a colloquium on comparable worth held at Rutgers University on October 9, 1987. The sessions were chaired by Anita Chaudhuri, Anne Marie Connell, Robert May, and Mary Merva, then graduate students in economics and political science at Rutgers. They not only directed the sessions but also made important contributions to the discussions that followed.

We are pleased to acknowledge the financial support of the Rutgers University Research Council, whose grant to the Graduate Program in Economics made the colloquium possible, and the assistance of the Department of Economics in facilitating scheduling and other arrangements. We are particularly grateful to Gauri Bijur and Dorothy Rinaldi for their assistance in organizing the colloquium and in preparing this book.

INTRODUCTION

Mark R. Killingsworth and M. Anne Hill

"EQUAL pay for jobs of comparable worth is destined to become one of the most hotly debated employment issues of the 1980's," stated the Bureau of National Affairs in 1981. Since then the comparable worth issue (or "pay equity," as it is sometimes called) has more than lived up to its advance billing.[1] It has been debated in Congress and state legislatures; it has been a central issue in numerous federal court cases; it played a role in the opposition by some groups to the nomination of Judge Anthony Kennedy to the U.S. Supreme Court; and it has led to sizable increases in pay for some state and municipal employees. Proponents sometimes argue that comparable worth will make the labor market function more efficiently; conversely, one newspaper editorial branded it "socialism in drag."

What Is Comparable Worth?

Comparable worth is a shorthand term for *equal pay for jobs of comparable worth*: the proposition that "comparable" jobs should receive the same pay. Comparability would generally be determined by a job evaluation in which points were assigned to jobs on the basis of skill, effort, responsibility, and working conditions; for example, a job with high skill or effort requirements or one that entailed unpleasant working conditions would receive more evaluation points than would other jobs. If two jobs turned out to have the same total point score, then,

---

1. In some cases, the terms *pay equity* and *comparable worth* are treated as synonymous; in other cases, *pay equity* is used as a general term denoting the absence of discrimination in pay, and *comparable worth* is treated as a specific means to that end.

even if they involved quite different duties (e.g., nurse and electrician), they would be said to be comparable and thus to merit the same rate of pay.[2]

There has been some disagreement (but, overall, not much discussion) concerning the details of a comparable worth policy. Advocates sometimes differ, for example, on how the points awarded for specific characteristics should be combined in arriving at the total point score for each job: Should points awarded for working conditions be given equal weight as points awarded for skill? If not, how should the weighting be done? Similarly, relatively little attention has been paid to technical issues regarding coverage: Would a comparable worth law cover literally all employers, or would some firms (e.g., ones with fewer than fifty workers) be exempt? Would job evaluations be undertaken on a companywide basis, even for multi-establishment firms with operations in many states; or would such evaluations be undertaken only within a single establishment?

On several matters, however, most proponents agree. First, job evaluations would be undertaken on an employer-by-employer (or even an establishment-by-establishment) basis; they would not entail interfirm comparisons, much less economywide comparisons, among jobs. Second, job evaluations at a given employer would be comprehensive and would definitely entail comparisons across occupational boundaries within the same firm. Finally, when two jobs were found to be comparable but to receive different rates of pay, compliance with the principle of equal pay for comparable worth would generally be achieved by raising the pay of the lower-wage job rather than, for example, reducing the pay of the higher-wage job or splitting the difference in the rates of pay.

As an example of how a prototype comparable worth policy might be implemented, suppose all the jobs at a given employer have been evaluated (e.g., by reviewing job descriptions, interviewing incumbents, and so on) and that evaluation points P are assigned to each job. The next step would be to determine whether jobs held predominantly by females are paid less than other jobs with the same number of evaluation points. This might be done by computing a regression of the form

---

2. The key difference between equal pay for jobs of comparable worth and equal pay for *equal work* is that, under the latter principle, jobs could be called "equal" only if they entailed essentially identical duties and functions (e.g., waiter and waitress). In contrast, a comparable worth standard would require equal pay for jobs found to be "comparable" (in terms of total point scores) even if their duties and functions were quite different (e.g., nurse and tree trimmer).

$$A_j = b_0 + b_F F_j + b_P P_j + e_j$$

where A is an administrative pay construct (e.g., the maximum, minimum, or midpoint of the pay range set for each job), F is a measure of the "femaleness" of the job,[3] P is the evaluation points awarded to the job,[4] e is a regression error term denoting unmeasured factors related to A, j indexes jobs, and the bs are the coefficients. If the estimate of b_F is negative and statistically significant at reasonable test levels, then jobs held predominantly by females are paid less than other jobs with the same number of evaluation points (P) and so are said to be paid significantly less than other jobs "of comparable worth." The predominantly female jobs might then be granted higher pay based on the magnitude of the estimated "femaleness effect," b_F.[5]

Background

Although job evaluation in the United States got its start in the late nineteenth century, interest in the comparable worth issue is relatively recent, stemming from concerns about the labor market status of women and the belief that existing laws and policies cannot adequately address the problems of women's labor market disadvantage.[6]

Sponsors of the 1963 Equal Pay Act explicitly rejected comparable worth in favor of the narrower principle of equal pay for equal work. Subsequent measures, including Title VII of the Civil Rights Act (passed the following year) and Executive Order 11246, focused on improving access to (better-paying) jobs rather than on changing the structure of pay for given jobs. Comparable worth continued to attract interest, however. In 1979, the Equal Employment Opportunity Commission commissioned the National Research Council's Commit-

---

3. For example, F might measure the proportion of incumbents in the job who are women—the "proportion female." Alternatively, F might be a binary indicator denoting whether the job is "predominantly female" (e.g., whether more than 70 percent of the incumbents in it are women).

4. P might be either the job's total point score or a vector, giving the scores awarded to the job for each of the individual factors (skill, effort, and so on) considered in the evaluation.

5. The nature of the adjustment would generally depend on how F was defined (recall n. 3). For example, if F is a binary indicator denoting "is a predominantly female job," the adjustment might entail a wage increase of $-b_F$ for all predominantly female jobs. If F is the proportion of a job's incumbents who are female, the adjustment might entail a wage increase of $-b_F F_j$ for job j (to eliminate the "femaleness component" in job j's pay rate, A_j) and would vary from one job to another.

6. Of course, comparable worth is also potentially relevant to minorities, but most discussions focus on its implications for women. See, for example, Treiman and Hartmann 1981, 9.

tee on Occupational Classification and Analysis to study the issue. The committee's report endorsed the concept in measured but unequivocal language:

> The committee is convinced by the evidence, taken together, that women are systematically underpaid. Policies designed to promote equal access to all employment opportunities will affect the underpayment of women workers only slowly . . . . the committee believes that the strategy of "comparable worth," that is, equal pay for jobs of equal worth, merits consideration as an alternative policy of intervention in the pay-setting process wherever women are systematically underpaid. (Treiman and Hartmann, 1981, 66–67)

Comparable worth has not fared well in the courtroom, however; on the whole, the federal courts have been either skeptical of or overtly hostile to the notion that unequal pay for "comparable" jobs, in the sense used by proponents of comparable worth, violates existing employment discrimination law.[7] Perhaps not surprisingly, therefore, few developments bearing on comparable worth have occurred in the private sector (*Wall Street Journal*, 1985, 1). In recent years, no private-sector employer has been sued in the federal courts on comparable worth grounds, and any pay agreements embodying comparable worth principles that may have been reached have not been publicized. Indeed, employer groups have frequently expressed opposition to comparable worth at congressional hearings.

Especially during 1984–88, the Reagan administration actively opposed comparable worth. The U.S. Department of Justice filed *amicus* briefs in opposition to the concept in several cases (e.g., *American Nurses Association*). In 1985, the U.S. Commission on Civil Rights voted to reject the doctrine of comparable worth by a five-to-two margin; shortly afterward, the five commissioners of the U.S. Equal Employment Opportunity Commission (EEOC) voted unanimously that federal law does not require employers to give equal pay for different jobs of comparable worth.

Partly as a result of this generally unencouraging reception on the part of the private sector, the federal courts, and the federal govern-

---

7. These cases include Christensen v. Iowa, 563 F.2d 353 (8th Cir. 1977); Briggs v. City of Madison, 536 F. Supp. 435 (W.D. Wis. 1982), *amended*, 28 F. E. P. 1795 (1983); Lemons v. City and County of Denver, 620 F.2d 228 (10th Cir. 1980); Spaulding v. University of Washington, 740 F.2d 686 (9th Cir. 1984); AFSCME v. State of Washington, 770 F.2d 1401 (9th Cir. 1985); American Nurses Ass'n v. State of Illinois, 783 F.2d 716 (7th Cir. 1986); and United Auto Workers v. State of Michigan, 673 F. Supp. 893 (E.D. Mich. 1988).

ment, proponents have focused their energies on state and local government employment. Here their efforts have met with greater success—as a result of negotiation (e.g., in Colorado Springs, Colorado); a strike (in San Jose, California); or legislative or administrative action (in, for example, state government employment in Iowa, Michigan, New York, and Minnesota and in municipal employment in Los Angeles).[8] Although no completely comprehensive survey exists, it appears that more than two-thirds of the fifty state governments have at least begun studies to determine whether compensation of state workers reflects the worth of their jobs and to consider (and in some cases to implement) changes to bring about a greater correspondence between a job's pay and its assessed worth. On several occasions since 1984, the U.S. Congress has considered bills requiring a study of federal civil service pay along comparable worth lines. The proposed legislation in each instance has passed the House of Representatives but has died in the Senate.

Papers in This Volume

Although the public debate about comparable worth has frequently generated substantial heat, it has not often generated much light. For the most part, both supporters and critics in the public arena have been concerned with advocacy, pro or con, rather than with careful analysis. In contrast, the papers in this volume attempt to assess the issues in a more serious fashion and to gauge the likely effects of adopting comparable worth.

One of the most important—and, to date, largely unexplored—issues in the comparable worth debate concerns the implications of different labor market structures. Many opponents base their arguments on simple models of supply and demand in the market and conclude that there is no substance to the view that unequal pay for jobs of comparable worth indicates discrimination: if jobs held predominantly by females are indeed "underpaid" relative to their "worth," why have profit-hungry employers not seized the opportunity to step up hiring for such positions, thereby increasing demand for, and thus the pay of, workers in such jobs?[9] Would it not be more reason-

---

8. Success has not always been complete, however. In many if not most instances (e.g., the cases of Minnesota and San Jose noted below), comparable worth advocates have sought and won pay adjustments, but the pay changes have been smaller than the ones necessary to provide literally equal pay for all jobs with the same worth, as measured by a job evaluation.

9. With only slight exaggeration, this view has been characterized as a statement that

able to conclude that so-called underpayment of such jobs is due to sex-related differences in job choices (due to sex role differentiation and differential socialization before entry into the labor market) than to discrimination by employers?

In contrast, most proponents of comparable worth reject simple supply-and-demand models of the labor market. In general, however, they have not rigorously analyzed whether, in alternative models of the labor market, sex-related differences in pay among jobs with the same evaluation points are meaningful evidence of employer discrimination.[10] Nor have they generally used these alternative models to examine the likely consequences of adopting a comparable worth standard.

In their paper for this volume, Mark Aldrich and Robert Buchele provide a detailed analysis of efficiency wage models—an important class of labor market models of relatively recent vintage—and consider their implications for the comparable worth debate. They argue that, in such models, the existence of sizable industry wage differentials unrelated to job attributes such as education or work experience may provide a justification for a comparable worth standard and that, to the extent that it enhances worker efficiency, adoption of comparable worth may have smaller effects on employment than have usually been contemplated. They add that the greatest impact of comparable worth might be in high-wage industries, where relatively few women are employed. If so, comparable worth might increase wage inequality among women even as it reduces wage disparities between men and women.

In her comment on Aldrich and Buchele, Marjorie Honig argues that although efficiency wage models can offer some insight into *interindustry* wage differentials, comparable worth would apply only to *intrafirm* differentials. Further, for the efficiency wage model to accommodate male-female wage differentials, men and women must exhibit different characteristics that are unrelated to productivity. Yet, if men and women are equally productive and women are paid less because of discrimination, nondiscriminatory firms that hire women at wages below men's will still be able to operate at lower costs and to drive discriminating firms out of the market.

---

the free market, unaided by any government intervention, is entirely capable of eradicating the discrimination that is not there.

10. The distinction is between necessary and sufficient conditions: Although employer discrimination may induce a negative relation between pay in occupations and the proportion of females in these occupations, it need not be the case that such a negative relation arises only because of such discrimination.

Charles H. Fay discusses the paper by Aldrich and Buchele from a human resource management perspective, challenging the view that the worth of a job can be determined independently of the market. In particular, he contends that the current approach in job evaluation is for a firm to appeal to the labor market in order to measure appropriately the intrafirm value of a job.

Joyce P. Jacobsen reaches conclusions generally less favorable to comparable worth than those in Aldrich and Buchele's analysis. She begins with the simplest possible supply-and-demand labor market model and then introduces various complications (e.g., interpersonal differences in skills and tastes and anticompetitive employer behavior). Jacobsen argues that in all these variants, adjusting wages via comparable worth tends to be undesirable on efficiency grounds but may lead to a more equal distribution of earnings.

Jacobsen speculates that increased enforcement of current antidiscrimination laws may be more effective than comparable worth in reducing the gender-based wage gap. Barbara A. Lee, a lawyer, argues in her comment on Jacobsen's paper that increased litigation is an "expensive, ineffective, and inefficient" means of closing that gap. In addition, Lee asserts, current laws fail to address two potential causes of the wage gap: crowding of women into low-paying jobs and the barriers faced by women seeking male-dominated jobs.

In her comment on Jacobsen, Rebecca M. Blank agrees with Lee that the potential of affirmative action to reduce the wage gap may be limited. Blank suggests an alternative means of raising wages in predominantly female occupations: unionizing the women in those jobs. Blank also notes a problem that policy makers may face in implementing a comparable worth wage policy: how will the administered wages be allowed to change as labor market conditions change? Finally, she argues that the supply-and-demand analysis that Jacobsen uses does not allow for an assessment of the potential effects of a comparable worth wage policy on the behavior of discriminatory employers. In particular, neoclassical economists have failed to specify adequately a theory of discrimination, especially regarding the formation of tastes by employers (and co-workers) for particular groups of workers.

Although both Aldrich and Buchele and Jacobsen touch on empirical questions, their primary focus is theoretical and analytical. Complementing these papers, those by Elaine Sorensen and Ronald G. Ehrenberg are concerned mainly with empirical issues.

One of the main issues in the comparable worth debate concerns the extent to which the male-female pay gap is affected by the difference in the distribution of men and women across occupations: because comparable worth wage adjustments are aimed at narrowing the difference in pay across occupational boundaries, their effects on the pay gap are likely to depend in an important way on the extent to which the pay gap results from male-female occupational differences.

Sorensen's paper focuses on the relationships among occupational characteristics, individuals' traits, and pay differences. After reviewing previous research, she presents new estimates based on the 1984 Panel Survey of Income Dynamics. She contends that previous research papers on this issue frequently suffer from methodological problems that raise doubts about their substantive conclusions. Hence, she argues, the existing literature on the relation between the pay gap and occupational differences by sex is inconclusive. Her own estimates imply that the sex composition of occupations accounts for a larger fraction of the pay gap than has been obtained in earlier work, suggesting that comparable worth may narrow the pay gap by more than has heretofore been expected.

Commenting on Sorensen, Judith M. Gerson advocates further research to identify the reasons underlying the negative relation between pay and the sex composition of jobs. She notes that at present we do not know whether decreases in (relative) wages drive men out of occupations or whether wages decline in anticipation of (or subsequent to) an influx of women workers. Although institutional models provide a potential alternative to conventional economic treatments, Gerson argues that such models do not explain the processes by which wage rates are set, but merely describe them. In particular, she says, such models have not adequately specified how customs, norms, and institutions affect individuals' decisions concerning occupational choice or employers' decisions about hiring or pay.

Claudia Goldin moves beyond Sorensen's empirical estimates of the negative relation between an occupation's sex composition and its wage to ask why such a relation might exist. To do so, she takes a historical perspective with a "pollution" theory of discrimination and considers changes in the labor market as women enter a market previously dominated by men. If women, on average, have a lower level of job-related human capital (e.g., "strength") than do men in a particular occupation, then men in that occupation may prefer not to work with women because entry of women will reduce the occupation's distribution of "strength" and hence its status. Yet, according to Goldin's model, the response of male incumbents in an occupation will depend on the average levels of human capital of the men and women in it: the presence of women may raise the status of some jobs and depress the status of others.

Ehrenberg's paper reviews the findings of research on the actual or expected effects of comparable worth in several areas, including not only the pay gap but also employment, female labor supply and occupational mobility, and general equilibrium effects. He considers not only ex ante studies—attempts to simulate what adoption of comparable worth might entail for the entire economy, for example, but also the relatively small number of ex post studies that have analyzed what happened when comparable worth was actually adopted in various jurisdictions (e.g., Iowa State government, San Jose municipal government). Although he notes that various methodological problems affect several of the analyses, he concludes that on the whole the studies (particularly the ex post studies) suggest that the actual effects of comparable worth would probably be fairly moderate: neither employment nor the wage gap (nor wage levels) seems to have changed dramatically. He cautions that very little is known about the second-round or induced effects of comparable worth on such labor market outcomes as occupational choices and the wage structure in the "uncovered" sector of the economy (i.e., the sector not directly affected by comparable worth wage adjustments).

In her comments on this paper, Janice Fanning Madden points out that although the estimates Ehrenberg reports of comparable worth reductions in the pay gap are "moderate" (on the order of 10 to 20 percent), these changes are large relative to historical movements in the gender wage gap. The ratio of women's to men's wages has changed by only about 15 percent during the last twenty-five years. Madden finds the differences between the public- and private-sector estimates of changes in the pay gap suggestive of potential problems that can result from aggregating across job titles and firms. Finally, Madden notes that although econometric and job evaluation models can yield information regarding the effect of gender on wages, these models cannot provide a unique hierarchical ranking of jobs. Implementing a comparable worth wage policy will ultimately require that wages be set through the political process.

Pamela Stone Cain, in her comments on Ehrenberg's paper, maintains that his conclusion—that the evidence indicates that comparable worth wage adjustments can narrow the wage gap—is significant. In contrast, she argues, empirical studies of the effects of affirmative action have generally been inconclusive. She also lists a number of issues on which further research is needed: How do political and logistical considerations affect actual comparable worth wage adjustments? Does using white male-dominated jobs to value particular job attributes cause a bias in the measured "worth" of other jobs and thus the wage adjustments awarded to such jobs? Do comparable worth wage adjustments affect productivity?

Outlook for the Future

The Bush administration is unlikely to foster a major shift in the attitude of the federal executive branch—the Justice Department, the EEOC, and the Civil Rights Commission—toward comparable worth. (The 1988 Republican platform explicitly opposed comparable worth.) And, given the importance of accumulating precedent, it seems unlikely that the federal courts will become more receptive to comparable worth in the near future.[11] As a result, large-scale implementation of comparable worth principles in the private sector in the next several years is unlikely.

Although prediction is hazardous, it follows that, at least for the near future, the public sector will continue to be the major battleground for proponents and opponents of comparable worth. States and municipalities will probably continue to debate the issue, conduct studies of their pay structures, and, in at least some significant instances, implement further comparable worth wage adjustments. At the national level, discussion is likely to be focused on proposals to conduct comparable worth studies of the federal pay structure, which, if adopted, are likely to lead to calls for comparable worth wage adjustments to the federal pay structure.

Thus the comparable worth issue will continue to be debated in the next decade. It is possible that future discussions will be characterized by less reliance on polemic and more emphasis on analysis and empirical evidence than has been the case to date. We believe that the papers and discussants' comments in this volume will raise the level of these debates, and may even influence their outcome.

---

11. The generally negative attitude of the federal courts toward comparable worth is likely to be consolidated by the recent elevation of Judge Anthony Kennedy to the U.S. Supreme Court: Judge Kennedy wrote an important appellate decision (*AFSCME v. State of Washington*; see n. 7 above) overturning a district court's judgment that the state of Washington discriminated against women by paying predominantly female jobs less than jobs that were predominantly male but otherwise comparable based on a job evaluation.

WHERE TO LOOK FOR COMPARABLE WORTH: THE IMPLICATIONS OF EFFICIENCY WAGES

Mark Aldrich and Robert Buchele

A DVOCATES of comparable worth reject the traditional supply-and-demand model of labor markets.[1] They envision a world in which large enterprises fill most of their jobs from internal labor markets, where wages are largely insulated from the forces of supply and demand and where markets need not clear. These internal labor markets are often structured along gender lines. Social norms concerning the appropriate roles for men and women are deeply embedded in the wage and job structure, and discriminatory hiring practices are enforced by "social, legal, cultural and economic conventions, including subtle pressures from family, employees, customers and 'the community' " (Strober 1984, 147).[2] Hence men and women

---

We wish to thank Roger Kaufman, Michele Naples, Elizabeth Savoca, and an anonymous referee for helpful comments on earlier drafts.

1. Contrast the advocate's vision Treiman and Hartmann present (1981, chap. 3) with Killingsworth's critique (1985b).

2. Bielby and Baron (1986) report on employer sex stereotyping of jobs (e.g., assigning men to jobs requiring physical strength and women to jobs requiring finger dexterity even though the strength and dexterity of the applicants could be cheaply and accurately assessed). And Kanter (1977, 197–98) reports that more than two-thirds of male executives polled by the *Harvard Business Review* said they would not feel comfortable working for a woman. Male-female differences in job "preferences" (whatever their origin) are certainly a factor here also. Marini and Brinton (1984, 200) report that the index of segregation of the occupational aspirations of a 1979 national sample of fourteen to twenty-two year olds was 61 percent. This is almost identical to the degree of occupational segregation that actually existed in the labor market according to Beller (1984, 14).

do not compete directly with one another for jobs in one big labor market, and "women's jobs" are underpaid relative to "comparable" "men's jobs." In view of the persistence of occupational segregation and low pay in many jobs dominated by women, despite market forces and public policies promoting equal opportunity and equal pay for women, comparable worth—equal pay for comparable work— emerges as a realistic and desirable public policy.

Some mainstream economists have also begun to question the supply-and-demand model of labor markets and have proposed instead various efficiency wage theories that have some resemblance to the views of comparable worth advocates. There are a number of such models, but they all share some common themes: there is nonprice rationing for "good" jobs, and labor markets do not clear. Substantial noncompensating wage differentials may exist for a given job (occupation) across firms and industries. Moreover, these are equilibrium differentials that are not eroded by competition. Finally, employee behavior (e.g., effort, propensity to quit) is endogenous: as in the classic Marxian formulation, the employer hires a worker's labor time; it is management's job to extract as much work as possible from the worker.

This paper briefly reviews several leading efficiency wage models, examines their implications for occupational segregation and occupational wage differentials, and evaluates their empirical support. We then estimate a comparable worth wage equation in which the effect on wages of the percentage female of an occupation (i.e., the percentage of workers in the occupation who are female) depends on the wage premium of the industry in which the occupation is located. Our results imply that the greatest potential for comparable worth wage adjustments is, ironically, in those high-wage industries in which relatively few women work.

Efficiency Wages and Women's Work

Efficiency wages are not a new idea; their modern revival was motivated by economists' efforts to explain involuntary unemployment: why is it that rational, profit-maximizing employers do not simply cut wages or replace existing employees when similarly skilled unemployed workers are willing to work for less than the current wage?[3]

---

3. The recent efficiency wage literature traces its origins to Leibenstein's (1957) argument that in underdeveloped countries labor productivity may depend positively on wages because higher wages improve workers' nutrition and stamina (Stiglitz 1986,

Attempts to explain this puzzle by appealing to efficiency wages have in turn led to a revival of interest in dual labor market models and —of most interest to us—to some new insights into labor market discrimination.

In the most general efficiency wage model, higher wages are assumed to elicit more effort per hour of labor, $E = E(w)$, in the manner shown in figure 2.1. The optimal wage, w^*, which minimizes labor costs per efficiency unit, $w/(E(w))$, satisfies the condition $E'(w)/[E(w)/w] = 1$—that is, there is unitary elasticity of effort with respect to the wage.[4] This result is illustrated in figure 2.1 by the tangency of the efficiency wage curve with a (unit elasticity) ray from the origin. With the optimal wage set, the employer hires labor up to the point where the marginal revenue product of labor equals w^*. The key result is that there is nothing in this model to ensure that the equilibrium, cost-minimizing wage, w^*, will clear the labor market.

In the "shirking" models of Shapiro and Stiglitz (1984) and Bulow and Summers (1986), effort is assumed to be a function of the cost (to the worker) of job loss and the risk of being discovered shirking and fired. If it is costly to monitor employee work activities (i.e., to detect shirking), firms may prefer to pay an above-market wage in order to raise the worker's cost of job loss and discourage shirking. In Bulow and Summers's model, equally productive workers may be employed either in primary jobs (where monitoring is costly) that pay efficiency wages to prevent shirking or in secondary jobs (where monitoring is costless) that do not. Bulow and Summers derive a "no-shirking condition" (NSC) that relates wages to primary-sector employment in essentially the following manner:

$$\frac{w_1 - w_2}{r} = \frac{a}{d} + \frac{aqN}{d(N - E_1)}.$$

Here, w_1 is the primary-sector wage and w_2 is the secondary-sector wage; d is the probability of being caught shirking and fired; q is the

---

182–83). Douglas (1934) traces intellectual interest in incentive pay systems to the 1890s.

4. See Stiglitz 1986. This result is derived as follows:

$$\frac{d}{dw}\left[w/E(w)\right] = E(w)^{-1} - wE(w)^{-2}[E'(w)] = 0$$

$$1 - wE(w)^{-1}[E'(w)] = 0$$

$$\frac{E'(w)}{E(w)/w} = 1$$

Figure 2.1.   Determination of the Efficiency Wage That Minimizes Labor
Cost per Efficiency Unit, w/E(w)

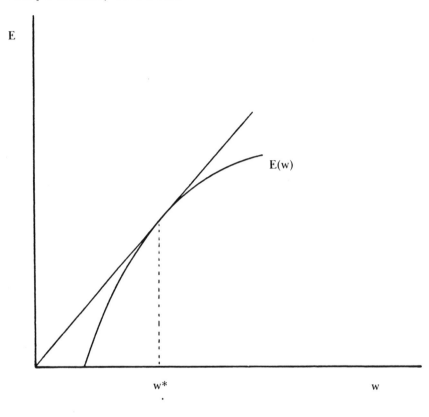

exogenous separation rate; a is the utility of shirking; and r is the
discount rate. Finally, N represents total employment and E_1
primary-sector employment. The NSC is graphed, along with the
primary-sector demand curve for labor (PDL), in figure 2.2. The result is primary-sector wages that exceed those in the secondary sector
for identical workers and queuing for high-wage primary-sector jobs.

This model can also generate occupational segregation if employers expect women workers to have higher quit rates than otherwise
similar men. If women have higher values for q, the NSC curve for
women will be above that for men, as shown in figure 2.3. If they
have higher exogenous separation rates, for any given E_1, women
must receive higher wages to be induced not to shirk. Hence, if we
assume that competition requires equal wages for all workers in
primary-sector jobs, equilibrium requires a relatively large proportion

Figure 2.2.   Equilibrium Wages and Primary-Sector Employment in the
Shirking Model

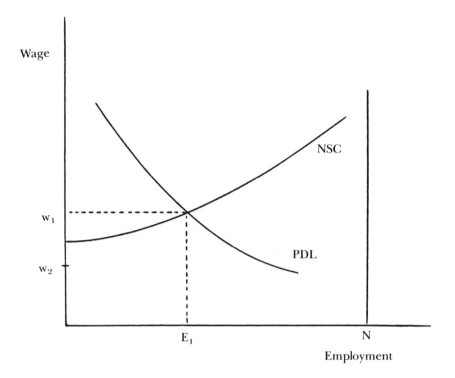

of women in secondary-sector jobs in order to prevent shirking (see
fig. 2.3).[5]

Although Bulow and Summers's model highlights certain features
of the labor market that are also stressed by comparable worth advocates, it provides no support for their favorite remedy. By raising
wages in the secondary sector, a comparable worth policy would raise
the no-shirking wage in the primary sector, thereby generating disemployment in both kinds of jobs.

___

5. A somewhat different version of the shirking model, attributable to Goldin
(1986), is specifically designed to explain occupational segregation and lower pay for
women. In Goldin's model, men are more responsive to deferred payment because
of their lower turnover rates. The result is that men are hired for jobs that are expensive to monitor and are paid a deferred wage to deter shirking, while women are hired
for jobs that are more easily monitored and are paid—net of monitoring costs—less
than equally productive men.

Figure 2.3.   Equilibrium Wage and Male and Female Employment in the Shirking Model

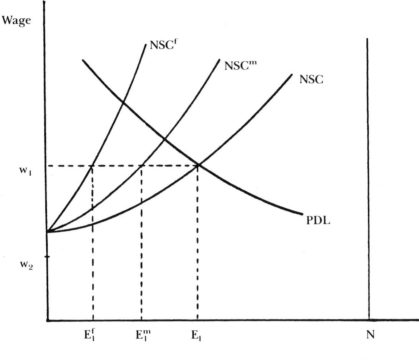

Another version of the efficiency wage model is based on the costs of turnover to the firm. Turnover costs are most important when there are large firm-specific training costs. But even when training costs are minimal, there are recruitment and hiring costs, and there may be losses in output when work groups are disrupted or when employees simply fail to show up for work. The effect of such costs is to reduce the net marginal product of labor, and in such situations firms may find it profitable to pay an above-market wage to reduce quits and absenteeism.

It is not hard to see how such a wage model could generate occupational segregation. If women have higher quit rates than men, employers will minimize turnover costs by hiring men before women. Women will be consigned to secondary jobs in which turnover is less costly, and they will not receive efficiency wages. Moreover, just as in Bulow and Summers's model, a comparable worth policy to raise wages in secondary-sector jobs will cause disemployment in both sectors.

Adverse selection models can also be deduced from the assumption that employers have imperfect information about potential new hires. Paying above-market wages may be profitable if it increases the quality of the applicant pool and reduces the probability that the best employees will quit. As one writer advising small construction contractors put it: "Paying 20 percent above average in wages will get you a 30 percent to 40 percent above-average employee" (Gerstel 1988, 70). Adverse selection models suggest the existence of statistical discrimination. When it is costly to evaluate individual job applicants, employers who believe that women as a group are more likely than men to quit will shun women in jobs with high turnover costs. The resulting exclusion of women from efficiency wage jobs gives rise to occupational segregation.

Samuel Bowles (1985) develops a Marxian model of the capitalist firm in which occupational segregation and pay discrimination occur under competitive conditions and are consistent with profit maximization. In this model workers may combine to resist employer surveillance efforts and to protect one another from employer sanctions for perceived malfeasance.[6] Employers can reduce unit costs by differentiating jobs, pay, and surveillance packages in order to undermine worker unity. This "divide-and-rule" strategy effectively exploits social divisions between whites and minorities and between men and women and fosters occupational segregation by race and sex. In this model discrimination is not simply costless, it is profitable. Profit-maximizing employers hire white men for some jobs, despite their higher wage costs, because this serves to segment the work force, undermine worker solidarity, and facilitate the extraction of labor from labor power.

Finally, we consider George A. Akerlof's (1982, 1984) sociological, or gift-exchange, model. In this analysis, workers respond to the "gift" of above-market wages with the "gift" of extra effort. Thus the

---

6. See Whyte 1955 for studies of work group resistance to monitoring and rate setting. Also see Gintis 1976 for a comparison of neoclassical and Marxian theories of the firm.

norm for group effort, E_n, depends on the group's wages, w, relative to some reference wage, w_r:

$$E_n = -c + b(w/w_r)^a.$$

This equation generates a function for the effort norm similar to the function for effort in figure 2.1. If individual effort depends on the norm for group effort, the efficiency wage (the wage that minimizes labor cost per unit of efficiency) can be an above-market wage and workers will queue for the "good jobs."

In Akerlof's model the reference wage is external to the firm; there is a dual labor market composed of primary-sector firms that pay above-market (efficiency) wages and secondary-sector firms that do not. But Akerlof's emphasis on group norms and equity issues, as well as Bowles's emphasis on job and wage segmentation and inequality within the firm, suggest the importance of a firm's internal wage structure to worker effort and to unit labor costs.

In fact, employers are generally concerned with both internal and external wage norms because departures from either can negatively affect employee effort and/or raise turnover costs. The fact that employers conduct job evaluations and concern themselves with the issue of internal equity supports advocates' contention that comparable worth does not entail a drastic departure from the current wage and salary policies of many large enterprises.[7] The larger and more insulated a firm is from product and labor market competition, the greater role job evaluation is likely to play in setting wages. Public employers, large firms in regulated and highly concentrated industries, and highly unionized firms are more likely to use job evaluation in setting wages than are smaller firms in competitive industries.[8]

Thus the novelty of comparable worth is not in its rejection of market wages but in its insistence on a common reference group for

7. Comparable worth, of course, emphasizes the importance of "internal equity" over external labor market supply-and-demand considerations. Some evidence in support of this perspective is found in Doeringer and Piore (1971), who report that the firms they studied placed more weight on job evaluation than on market wage surveys in setting wages, and in the claim of a former compensation director at Eastman Kodak that "there is always some degree of conflict between internal and external pay equity. The position taken by most salary administrators is that internal relationships should be given first priority and external pay relationships for certain jobs must be compromised on occasion" (Katz 1986, 249).

8. Recent trends toward deregulation, increased international competition, and declining unionization rates may be bringing wages back into competition in some formerly "sheltered" industries. The industry wage premiums found by Katz (1986) and others, however, indicate that firms do not simply "match the market."

blue- and white-collar jobs. In the advocates' view, comparable worth is just job evaluation "writ large." But the problem of reconciling internal pay norms based on job evaluation and external pay norms based on market wage surveys is obviously compounded in the case of comparable worth, in which a single job-rating scheme is applied to a much wider range of jobs. Hence comparable worth at present represents a radical—and no doubt costly—revision in most existing job evaluation schemes. The models proposed by Bowles and Akerlof, however, imply that a comparable worth campaign that changed group norms about the relative worth of women's jobs might be successful even if it was not enacted into law. By inducing women to compare their wages and job points with the wages and job points in men's jobs rather than with those in other women's jobs, it could raise employers' optimal wage for jobs held by women.[9]

Evidence on Efficiency Wages

Roger T. Kaufman (1984), in his survey of twenty-six firms in economically depressed areas of Great Britain, found that wage cutting or replacement of existing workers with qualified job applicants who would work at a lower wage was ruled out—even by small, nonunion firms—because employers felt it would have a deleterious effect on workers' morale, goodwill, and productivity. While Kaufman's interviews show that individual employers may pay above-market wages for reasons of X-efficiency, others have sought evidence of efficiency wages in the existence of industry wage premiums. There is a great deal of evidence that persistent noncompensating wage differentials for a given job exist between industries. Dunlop (1957, 135), for example, has shown that the average wages of unionized delivery truck drivers in Boston varied from $1.28 (for laundry delivery) to $2.39 (for newspaper delivery).

More contemporary data also show wide variation in individual earnings, even after other influences have been controlled. Table 2.1 reports Lawrence F. Katz's (1986) estimates of one-digit industry wage differentials based on 1983 Current Population Survey data. According to these estimates, workers in mining are paid 29 percent more than average, whereas workers in retail trade are paid 16 per-

---

9. Zanna, Crosby, and Loewenstein (1987, 31) report on a survey that showed 60 percent of all women in high-prestige jobs and 86 percent of all women in low-prestige jobs compared themselves to other women in "trying to decide how good [their] own job is." More than 93 percent of all men (in either high- or low-prestige jobs) compared themselves to other men.

Table 2.1.   Estimated Industry Wage Differentials for One-Digit Industries

Industry	*Wage Differential*
Mining	28.9%
Construction	12.7
Nondurable manufacturing	5.0
Durable manufacturing	9.8
Transport, communications, and public utilities	15.4
Wholesale trade	4.2
Retail trade	-16.1
Finance, insurance, and real estate	5.2
Services	-6.4

SOURCE: Katz 1986, 245. Controls include education, experience, sex, race, part-time work, marital status, unionization, standard metropolitan statistical area (SMSA), and eleven occupational and fifty state dummies.

cent less, even after differences in human capital, occupational mix, region, race and sex composition, and unionization rates are controlled. Moreover, such differentials persist even when more disaggregated industries are used. Nor can they be explained by appeals to unmeasured human capital, for job switchers who enter high-wage industries see their earnings go up while those who enter low-wage industries see them decline (Krueger and Summers 1986).

In most of the models described above, efficiency wages are paid where the cost to the firm of worker malfeasance, shirking, or turnover is high, monitoring costs are high, and employment is stable. Although most of these job characteristics are probably more closely related to occupation than to industry, certain industry characteristics might lead to the payment of efficiency wages. Employers in capital-intensive industries, for example, in which profits depend on undisrupted production and high capacity utilization rates, may be particularly concerned about worker malfeasance, absenteeism, and quitting. The size of the establishment may affect ability to monitor employees, and exceptionally profitable firms, often found in concentrated industries, might be under normative pressures to "share the wealth." Furthermore, many of these industry characteristics are associated with the presence of unions, and unions, or the threat of unionization, may provide an additional force to pay higher wages.

Insider-outsider models provide an alternative, but complementary, explanation for industry wage differentials (see Lindbeck and Snower 1986 and 1988). These models assume that current employees (insiders) are in a position to make it costly for employers to hire new employees (outsiders) at lower wages by refusing to cooperate and otherwise making it unpleasant for them. Thus the ability insiders have to raise turnover costs gives them bargaining power that they can use to appropriate part of an employer's monopoly rents.

Though only certain jobs might justify an efficiency wage strategy to reduce turnover or shirking, normative considerations ("fairness") might dictate higher wages for other jobs in a firm even when there is no technical basis for them (Akerlof and Yellen 1988). If intrafirm relative wage comparisons are as important to workers as many personnel administrators and students of internal labor markets believe, one might expect industry wage differentials to be fairly highly correlated across occupations.

Katz (1986, 261) presents evidence that, controlling for the differences in job and worker characteristics listed in the note on table 2.1, three-digit industry wage differentials are highly correlated across one-digit occupations. The correlation between managers' and laborers' industry wage differentials is 0.81, for example, and the correlation between clerical and operative wage differentials is 0.76. This finding is inconsistent not only with most efficiency wage models but with the theory of compensating wage differentials and the union threat effects model, for none of them predicts that wage differentials should be highly correlated across, for example, blue- and white-collar jobs. This finding is consistent, however, with the idea that there is considerable rigidity in a firm's occupational wage structure and that industry wage premiums in certain jobs—whatever their source—give rise to similar premiums in other jobs.

Little direct evidence exists on whether or not industry wage premiums are justified by enhanced worker efficiency. Both Krueger and Summers (1986) and Leonard (1987) present evidence that quit rates depend on industry wage levels. But in neither case is the relationship strong enough to make the wage premium economic (the estimated wage premium is many times larger than any potential saving from reduced turnover). Krueger and Summers show that a number of measures of job satisfaction depend positively on the wage level, but there is little hard evidence that job satisfaction and productivity are related. Leonard estimates occupational wages as a function of supervisory intensity and finds little evidence of the negative coefficient predicted by the shirking model.[10]

---

10. The best known case study of what looks like an efficiency wage policy is Henry Ford's famous five-dollar day, introduced in 1914. Why Ford dropped this bombshell is not entirely clear, but from an efficiency wage perspective it does not seem to have panned out. The five-dollar day just about doubled daily labor costs at Ford. As efficiency wage theories suggest, it also seems to have drastically reduced labor turnover. Raff and Summers (1986) and Raff (1988), however, conclude that the reduction in

As shown earlier, the exclusion of women from efficiency wage jobs might be explained by male-female differences in turnover rates. But the evidence that women have higher quit rates is mixed. W. Kip Viscusi (1980) found that women quit more often than men during their first year on a new job but that after the first year they have the same quit rates. James F. Ragan and Sharon Smith (1981) report that women's quit rates are higher than men's (20.4 percent versus 14.8 percent per year) in their sample. Francine D. Blau and Lawrence Kahn (1981) studied a sample of workers in which uncontrolled quit rates were 33 percent per year for women and 23 percent per year for men. The addition of wage, personal characteristics, and job-related controls eliminated the difference, however, and the marginal impact of wages in reducing turnover was higher for women than for men.[11] Finally, in a sample in which men and women had virtually identical uncontrolled quit rates, Mark E. Meitzen (1986) found that the difference between the top wage in the employee's job class and in the local labor market wage had a larger (negative) effect on women's quit rates than on men's. Such evidence provides limited support for efficiency wage models that assume higher quit rates among females in order to explain the occupational segregation and low wages of women.

Sex differences in the wage elasticity of effort might also explain the exclusion of women from efficiency wage jobs. A study by Thomas N. Daymont and Paul Andrisani (1984), for example, found that in a survey of high school seniors (class of 1972) males were twice as likely as females (22 versus 11 percent) to state that making money was a very important consideration in choosing a job. In contrast, women were more likely than men to state that opportunities to help others (72 versus 42 percent) and to work with people rather than things (68 versus 40 percent) were very important considerations. Such findings suggest that employers would prefer to hire men over women for jobs in which efficiency wages are used to motivate workers simply because men are more sensitive to monetary incentives. This could result in job segregation (in which women are excluded

---

turnover costs probably saved no more than 16 percent of the wage increase. There were, in addition, sharp productivity gains, possibly due to the relative rise in Ford's wages. Estimates made by contemporaries plus those of Raff and Summers suggest that higher wages may have led to at most a 40 to 70 percent rise in labor productivity. Raff concludes that Ford was trying to buy labor peace by sharing his rents with the workers.

11. Because workers may be sorted into different kinds of jobs on the basis of their different quitting behavior, male-female differences in quit rates are not ruled out by evidence that their quit rates are the same when differences in job characteristics are controlled.

from efficiency wage jobs) and lower wages in jobs dominated by women rather than men.

But other outcomes are possible. As the hedonic wage model suggests, effort could be elicited by increasing any favorable job trait (or reducing any unfavorable one). Thus women might be paid less but would not necessarily be excluded from "efficiency" jobs if effort could be elicited by improving the unfavorable job traits. The result would be segregation by firm (men or women hired for a certain job depending on the employer's job design) but not necessarily by industry or occupation.

In sum, current efficiency wage literature cannot satisfactorily account either for large and persistent noncompensating industry wage differentials or for occupational sex segregation. (The Marxian and sociological models are largely untested, however.) As a result, some authors have proposed that unexplained wage differentials reflect rent sharing by employers with their labor force (Krueger and Summers 1987).

There is direct evidence that employers with market power do pay above-market wages and are more likely than competitive firms to practice occupational sex segregation. But little is known about how market power affects the firm's occupational wage structure.[12] In the following section, we hypothesize that industry wage premiums result partly from rent sharing. Because of the "social, legal, cultural, and economic conventions" that advocates stress (Strober 1984, 147), the rent gets shared primarily with employees in male-dominated jobs. This conclusion suggests that the impact of comparable worth depends crucially on the industry in which it is implemented.

---

12. Some tests have supported Becker's (1957) hypothesis that employers with market power have more latitude to exercise employment discrimination than employers operating in competitive product markets. Ashenfelter and Hannan (1986), for example, found that women held 25 percent of the positions of bank officers and managers in the most highly concentrated markets in their sample, whereas women held 30 percent of those positions in the least highly concentrated markets. Haessel and Palmer (1978) found a tendency for firms in more concentrated industries to engage more heavily in sex typing, as shown by their greater preference for women in clerical and personal service jobs and for men in jobs more traditionally held by men. These findings suggest that the share of women in an occupation depends on the market structure of the industry in which the job is found.

With respect to the effect of market power on wages, Weiss (1966) found that the earnings of male operatives were higher in concentrated industries but that this was explained by the higher quality of the labor. More recent studies have shown that workers in concentrated and regulated industries receive wage premiums that cannot be completely accounted for by the higher quality of the labor (Dalton and Ford 1977; Shackett and Trapani 1987) and that "concentration, plant size, and unionization all exercise significant and independent effects on wages" (Kwoka 1983, 251).

Table 2.2.   Industry Wage Differentials and Employment Distribution

Industry	Wage Differential	Distribution Men	Distribution Women	Percentage Female
Mining	.289	1.88%	.35%	13.5%
Construction	.127	11.36	1.26	8.5
Durable manufacturing	.098	17.26	7.32	26.2
Nondurable manufacturing	.050	9.37	8.43	43.0
Transport, communications, and public utilities	.154	9.58	4.07	26.2
Finance, insurance, and real estate	.052	4.82	7.95	57.9
Wholesale trade	.042	5.91	2.80	28.4
Retail trade	-.161	16.05	22.24	53.7
Services	-.064	23.76	45.58	61.6
All		100.00%	100.00%	45.6%

SOURCE: Industry wage differentials are from table 2.1. Employment data pertain to private-sector nonagricultural workers, calculated from *Current Population Report*, series P-60 (Bureau of the Census, U.S. Department of Commerce), March 1983.

Industry Wage Premiums and Comparable Worth

There is good evidence that the overrepresentation of women workers in low-wage industries (and perhaps firms) is an important source of the gender gap in earnings. This is suggested by the data in table 2.2, which show that two-thirds of all women (versus two-fifths of all men) employed in the private, nonagricultural sector work in retail trade and services, the two industry groups with negative wage differentials according to Katz's estimates. Conversely, almost 23 percent of all men (versus less than 6 percent of all women) are employed in the three industry groups with the largest wage premiums (mining, construction and transport, communications and public utilities). Thus large positive differentials are associated with predominantly male labor forces, while negative wage differentials are associated with predominantly female labor forces.

Econometric studies also support the contention that industry characteristics matter. Randy Hodson and Paula England (1986), for example, find that capital intensity and degree of unionization in a (three-digit) industry account for about 15 percent of the male-female pay gap, but they find no net effect, controlling for industry and personal characteristics, of percentage female in the industry on men's and women's wages. Thus women earn less than men in part because they are concentrated in low-wage industries, but these industries are not low wage because women are crowded into them.

George Johnson and Gary Solon (1986) show that the wage gap between virtually all-male and all-female jobs is reduced by 46 percent for men and by 35 percent for women by the addition of twenty industry dummies.

Johnson and Solon's estimates provide an indication of the *average* effect of comparable worth across different industries. The inverse relationship between an industry's percentage female and its wage premium (table 2.2) suggests that their estimates could be the result of a minimal effect in some industries and a substantial one in others.

To explore this possibility, we have estimated wage equations that make the impact of the percentage female in an occupation conditional on the size of the industry wage premium. The equations thus include the percentage female in the worker's occupation (PFM), the wage premium associated with the worker's industry (IWP), and the interaction of these two variables (PFWP = PFM * IWP). We hypothesize that the coefficient of PFM is negative (the negative effect on wages of the percentage female) and the coefficient of IWP is positive (the positive effect on the wages of individual workers of industry wage differentials). Finally, if industry wage premiums include some rent sharing and if such sharing is limited largely to male-dominated jobs, the coefficient of PFWP should be negative.

We combine men and women in a single equation because we seek a single wage adjustment for all workers in an occupation (rather than a different one for the males and the females). The percentage female in the occupation is our quantitative measure of the occupation's gender. To obtain an estimate of its effect (i.e., the comparable worth effect) net of the effect of the gender of the individual, we include a sex dummy to control for the latter. Our wage correction thus conforms to the comparable worth practice of addressing only interoccupational wage discrimination and giving all workers in the same occupation the same wage adjustment. These equations also contain controls for race, human capital, job requirements, and location (see note in table 2.3 for a description of the controls).

The results reported in table 2.3 indicate that, after controlling for worker and job characteristics but not for industry wage differentials, there is a $1.19 per hour wage gap between virtually all-male occupations and virtually all-female occupations. Evaluated at the mean of all other independent variables, this gap implies that there is a 19 percent wage differential between the jobs dominated completely by men and those dominated by women. This differential shrinks to $.53 (or 7.9 percent) when industry wage differentials and the interaction term are added to the equation. The industry wage premium and its interaction with the percentage female both have a large,

Table 2.3.   Wage Equations: Regression Coefficients
(t-statistics in parentheses)

Independent Variable	Equation 1	Equation 2
PFM	-1.19	-0.53
	(5.19)	(2.29)
IWP	—	5.52
		(9.55)
PFWP	—	-2.61
		(2.62)
Standard error of the equation	2.81	2.74
R^2	.398	.427
n 2,990		

NOTE: The equations also contain controls for sex, race, schooling, work experience, job tenure, education, and training requirements of the job as measured by general educational development and specific vocational preparation, region, and SMSA. Industry wage differentials are estimated by Krueger and Summers (1987, table 2.1). They are net industry effects, controlling for labor quality and personal characteristics of the workers in the industries. All other data are from the National Longitudinal Surveys of Young Men and Young Women (1980) and the *Dictionary of Occupational Titles* (1977). See Aldrich and Buchele 1986, chaps. 3 and 4, for a complete description of these data.

statistically significant effect on wages. The positive effect of IWP indicates that working in an industry with a positive (negative) wage differential raises (or lowers) a worker's wage. The negative interaction term indicates that the wage penalty on female-dominated jobs (and thus the comparable worth wage correction) is greater in high-wage industries than in low-wage industries.

Table 2.4 uses equation 2 in table 2.3 to calculate the industry wage differential in typical male-dominated and female-dominated occupations (part A) and a representative comparable worth wage adjustment in high-, medium-, and low-wage industries (part B). Estimates in part A indicate that, controlling for productivity-related differences, workers in male-dominated jobs are paid $1.50 per hour (or 24 percent) more in high-wage industries than in low-wage industries. In female-dominated jobs, the differential is $1.11 per hour (or 18 percent).

In part B of table 2.4 we see that the comparable worth effect—specifically, the net effect of an occupation being 70 percent female versus 20 percent female—on its wage is $.46 per hour (6.3 percent) in high-wage industries (those paying a 15 percent wage premium), $.27 per hour (4.0 percent) in zero wage premium industries, and $.07 per hour (1.1 percent) in low-wage industries (those with a 15

Table 2.4.   Wage Gap between High- and Low-Wage Industries
and between Men's and Women's Jobs

	Dollars	Percentage
A. Wage Gap between High- and Low-Wage		
Industries		
Men's jobs	$1.50	24.1%
Women's jobs	1.11	18.0
B. Wage Gap between Men's and Women's Jobs		
In high-wage industries	.46	6.3
In zero wage premium industries	.27	4.0
In low-wage industries	.07	1.1

SOURCE: Calculated from equation 2 in table 2.3 assuming that high- and low-wage industries have plus and minus 15 percent wage differentials, respectively, and that typical men's jobs are 80 percent male and that typical women's jobs are 70 percent female.

percent wage penalty). Thus comparable worth appears to have the greatest impact in high-wage industries—those associated with a large wage premium in table 2.2. Unfortunately for comparable worth advocates, relatively few women are employed in these industries.[13] These results suggest that comparable worth would primarily benefit a relatively small number of women workers who already enjoy a substantial industry wage premium. If this is the case, comparable worth could actually increase wage inequality among women even as it reduced wage inequality between workers in male- and female-dominated jobs.

Conclusion

The efficiency wage literature reinforces some conclusions derived from supply-and-demand economics, but it also provides fresh in-

---

13. As table 2.2 shows, in 1983 only 13 percent of all women employed in the private sector worked in mining, construction, durable goods manufacturing, or transportation, communications, and public utilities—the only industries with a wage premium of 10 percent or more. And, although the great majority of those women worked in female-dominated occupations, certainly not all did. This analysis excludes government because no industry wage premium data were available for the public sector. Government is a major sector of employment for females and a focus of comparable worth activity. Although it is not a notably high-wage sector, it probably has more in common with high-wage premium industries than with low-wage premium industries. Specifically, it is less competitive and more regulated and more highly unionized than the low-wage sector. Thus the arena for potentially fruitful comparable worth campaigns is considerably wider than this discussion implies.

sights into sex discrimination and comparable worth. On a theoretical level some of the efficiency wage models yield the human capital prediction that occupational segregation and low wages in female-dominated jobs are attributable to differences between men's and women's tastes and labor force attachments. But unlike more orthodox models, some of the efficiency wage literature also implies that discrimination may sometimes be costless to employers. Moreover, models such as Akerlof's suggest that if women begin to compare their earnings with those in "comparable" male-dominated jobs, employers may voluntarily implement comparable worth in order to maintain morale and productivity.

Perhaps the most important contribution of the efficiency wage literature to the discussion of sex discrimination has been to return our attention to the existence of large industry wage differentials. These differentials appear to reflect rent sharing with certain groups of workers as well as possible payments to reduce turnover or shirking. The idea of discriminatory rent sharing suggests that the insider-outsider model, modified to allow only certain insiders (primarily those in male-dominated jobs) the bargaining power to appropriate monopoly rents, could be a useful framework for further research on interindustry differences in the impact of comparable worth.

Our findings suggest that the greatest potential for comparable worth is in industries that pay substantial wage premiums: the femaleness of a job has a substantial impact on wages in industries with large wage premiums and virtually no impact in industries with negative wage differentials. Unfortunately, a comparable worth policy that focused on high-wage industries and forced employers to share with workers in female-dominated jobs the rents that have historically been reserved for men would benefit relatively few women. At the same time, such a redistribution of rents might have even smaller disemployment effects than have been estimated by neoclassical substitution models.

DISCUSSION

MARJORIE HONIG

This discussion of efficiency wage models, while useful, is puzzling in the context of the comparable worth argument. Efficiency wages are offered as an explanation of *interindustry* wage differentials. Comparable worth, however, is proposed as a solution to *intrafirm* wage differences.

There are two possible explanations for this juxtaposition of efficiency wages and comparable worth. Either there is some confusion in the comparable worth arena, or, alternatively, proponents may hope to extend the coverage to interindustry differentials, the current focus of the discussion on the firm notwithstanding. In my opinion, this is neither feasible nor desirable. Regardless, the implication of the efficiency wage argument in this case, if correct, is clear: any compression of interindustry differentials in the spirit of comparable worth would be inadvisable because it would reduce primary-sector employment of women (and men) by raising the efficiency wage premium.

The paper suggests that the main value of the efficiency wage argument is to focus attention on interindustry differentials as a source of the gender-based wage gap. Several studies have already convincingly demonstrated the importance of such differences. It appears, in fact, that the major sources of gender-based wage differentials are both interindustry and interfirm. In this case, the internal wage structure argument advanced by advocates of comparable worth, even if correct, may address only a small part of the problem. Comparable worth legislation, in other words, may be a feeble mechanism for dealing with the problem at hand, a conclusion reached by this paper as well. The author's findings imply that the greatest potential for comparable worth may be in industries that pay efficiency wages. They point out, however, that there are few women in these industries.

For efficiency wages to generate gender-based wage differentials, there must be differences between men and women, such as differential quit rates, that are not related to productivity. As the authors note, however, the evidence on quit rates by gender is mixed. They cite studies indicating that turnover rates do not differ by gender after controlling for job characteristics. This is not inconsistent with the efficiency wage argument. As the model implies, workers in jobs with a high turnover will be assigned by the market to certain categories of jobs. It is therefore not appropriate in this case to control for job characteristics.

The paper suggests that the efficiency wage model may imply costless (i.e., persistent) discrimination: a queue for primary-sector jobs allows employers to select men exclusively, at zero cost. This is not correct. If men and women are equally productive and women are paid less because of discrimination, nondiscriminating firms may offer women lower wages than men without fear of their shirking because the opportunity wages for women are lower. Nondiscriminating firms will achieve lower costs, and competition will drive out discriminating firms.

CHARLES H. FAY

I come as a discussant for this paper with some trepidation: I am not
an economist but a human resource management specialist by training. Studies in human resource management, and particularly in
compensation issues, require a grounding in economics, but that
grounding has to compete with similar requirements in the fields
of industrial psychology, law, organizational behavior, and systems
management.

I also have an abiding interest in the practical, for human resource
management is a professional rather than a strictly academic field. I
think it may be useful to describe what human resource managers,
and particularly compensation managers, would like from economists,
and particularly from economists who advocate comparable worth.
When academics make suggestions for practices in organizations, and
particularly for practices that affect workers as much as changes in
individual pay levels do, there is a clear responsibility to understand
current practices and the reasons those practices exist.

John T. Dunlop (1957) referred to the "task of contemporary wage
theory." I believe that much of that task still remains to be accom-
plished; a basis for determining the value of a job to an organization
still needs to be developed. The issue of comparable worth (that is,
that jobs whose value to the organization is comparable should be
paid comparably), while rejected almost universally by compensation
professionals, would make a valuable contribution if it served as a
spur to the completion of the economist's (and other compensation
theorists') task.

I have a gut feeling, for example, that nurses really ought to make
more than parking meter repairers or tree trimmers, regardless of
the findings of the judge in *Lemons v. City and County of Denver* (620
F.2d 228 (10th Cir. 1980)). What I need to justify that feeling is some
basis for measuring the value to the organization of any individual
job, be it nurse or tree trimmer or even economist. I would be pleased
to learn of some conceptual foundation that could serve as the basis
for such a measure. So far, the market is the sole basis for measuring
value.

Even with a sales job, for example, the market is the final measure
of value. It may be possible to allocate overhead and other sales ex-
penses accurately and to determine precisely how much net profit the
salesperson has contributed to the organization. (I might note that
few sales compensation experts would argue that this is possible.) But
even then, except by reference to the market, one would still not

know how much of the net profit generated must go to the sales representative and how much the organization can keep. It is not by chance that most commercial wage survey organizations offer one or more surveys of sales compensation.

What economics could contribute to compensation practice is the development of a conceptual foundation that would help compensation professionals determine appropriate rates for individual jobs. Such an accomplishment would do much more than merely achieve internal gender-related pay equity; it would provide the basis for a rational and effective pay program.

Marjorie Honig has described in her comments some problems in efficiency wage theory from an economist's point of view, and to a noneconomist they seem cogent and well argued. My comments will focus on the degree to which Aldrich and Buchele's arguments reflect current compensation practice and provide a conceptual foundation that a compensation manager so disposed might use to correct a gender-related (or any other) pay inequity.

Much of Aldrich and Buchele's argument with respect to efficiency wages rests to some extent on two contentions: that for most organizations wage structures are developed on the basis of some accurate measure of the value of a job, as captured by a job evaluation system, and that the internal wage structure takes precedence over market rates. The first contention has never been true; the second, while it may at one time have been true, is not so today.

Organizations today develop pay structures using one of two basic approaches: market pricing and traditional job evaluation.

Under market pricing schemes, job attributes are collected for all jobs. In most cases traditional job evaluation variables (e.g., training required, education, responsibility, working conditions) are used, although not always. Some organizations, for example, use any quantified job analysis information that is available, such as Position Analysis Questionnaire (PAQ) profiles (Mecham and McCormick 1969). The organization also collects as much information on market wages as possible. As organizations face stiffer competition in product markets, they have tended to try to develop data more aligned with industry and location characteristics. (See Fay 1987 for the impact this is having on pay practices.) Market wages are then regressed on job attributes. The company pays the market wage when such information is available or, when such information is not available, the best estimate of what the market would pay.

My analysis of survey data from about 1,500 private-sector organizations (Risher and Fay 1988) indicates that market pricing is the predominant form of job pricing in the United States today; 60 percent of the surveyed organizations reported market pricing as the basis for determining wage levels for one or more job classifications. (For a more detailed description of market pricing strategies, see Fay's article "External Pay Relationships.")

Under more traditional job evaluation schemes, the organization builds a value hierarchy of jobs based on the degree to which jobs possess selected attributes, or compensable factors. Selected "key" jobs (representing those that account for a significant portion of the payroll of the organization *and* that are thought to be relatively stable with respect to technology and *fairly priced in the marketplace*) are priced in the market, and those market wages are manipulated (e.g., averaged) to develop a base wage for each salary grade. (A more detailed explanation of job evaluation practices is available in Wallace and Fay 1988 or Treiman 1979.)

Even in traditional job evaluation schemes (as noted in Schwab 1984, Milkovich 1984, and most other compensation theorists), job evaluation is simply a means of rationalizing market wages—when job evaluation results and market data are at odds the market almost always takes precedence—on both the up and the down side. Salary structures are typically revised annually to reflect market levels and changes in the market relationships between jobs. Jobs with high turnover rates are typically repriced sooner, if pay is thought to be a problem.

Doeringer and Piore (1971) and Katz (1986) notwithstanding, the compensation administration literature does not emphasize the importance of the internal wage structure over the market wage—and as organizations come under even more competitive pressure compensation managers are placing increasingly more emphasis on paying no more than can be justified by comparison with the wages of product market competitors for the same job.

The contention by Aldrich and Buchele that because "employers conduct job evaluations and concern themselves with the issue of internal equity supports advocates' [of comparable worth] contention that comparable worth does not entail a drastic departure from the current wage and salary policies of many large enterprises" is not supported by data or logic. Current compensation theory and practice bolsters the supply-and-demand criticism of comparable worth. In fact, the growing emphasis on product market (rather than labor market) competitors as the appropriate wage survey match suggests that notions of labor demand as a derived demand have begun to affect practice.

Aldrich and Buchele are equally incorrect (or, perhaps, comparably incorrect) in arguing that the "novelty of comparable worth is not in its rejection of market wages but in its insistence on a common reference group for blue- and white-collar jobs." Given current compensation practices, the rejection of market wages is novel indeed—much more novel than applying the same job-pricing scheme to both blue- and white-collar jobs. In a survey of 1,500 organizations (Risher and Fay 1988), 70 percent of the respondents reported using the same job evaluation process for executives as for middle management, 68 percent reported using the same job evaluation process for both sales representatives and scientists and engineers as for middle management, 96 percent used similar systems for both exempt support staff and for middle management, *57 percent used the same systems for both clerical employees and middle management, and 30 percent used the same systems for hourly employees and middle management.* (The focus job category of the survey was middle management; results reported here do not include the use of the same system for any other two job categories.) If instituting comparable worth required only the use of the same job evaluation system across job classes, then gender-based wage differentials would be much smaller today than those observed.

It is simply not the case that "comparable worth is just job evaluation writ large." Comparable worth implies that jobs have some true "worth" waiting to be discovered. In fact, for the majority of compensation professionals, jobs have no worth outside the context of the market.

The second issue I wish to address is the usefulness of efficiency wage theory if it is to reflect practice and how a compensation manager might use it as a guide for such practice. It could be argued that this is not an appropriate criterion for economic analysis. The advocates of comparable worth have argued in court, however, that notions of comparable worth should guide (rule) practice. Thus the usefulness of Aldrich and Buchele's paper is both a fair and necessary criterion.

Aldrich and Buchele suggest that the most important contribution of the efficiency wage literature is to "return our attention to the existence of large industry wage differentials." In fact, the attention of practitioners has never veered far from industry practices; virtually all wage surveys have industry breakouts, and many industry associations sponsor their own surveys. The notion of wage contours has guided practice since Dunlop published his article "The Task of Contemporary Wage Theory" (1957). The growing influence of business planning and strategy, with its emphasis on product market competition, on all human resource management practices is reflected in the attention paid to industry practices by most compensation managers.

Practitioners, but not advocates of comparable worth, may find comfort in this assertion by Aldrich and Buchele: "The greatest potential for comparable worth is in industries that pay substantial wage premiums . . . . unfortunately, a comparable worth policy that focused on high-wage industries and forced employers to share with workers in female-dominated jobs the rents that have historically been reserved for men, would benefit relatively few women." I'm not sure, however, what the compensation manager could do with that.

The pressure for comparable worth adjustments has come largely from lower-wage industries: health care, government, financial services (e.g., banking), and retailing. Are women in these industries to forget about comparability adjustments? How would the compensation manager in a high-wage industry determine the degree to which the salaries in male-dominated jobs are composed of "rents" as opposed to "true value"? Should women who are successful in male-dominated jobs have their salaries reduced by the same rent-control mechanism as male incumbents?

While it is clear that women are discriminated against in their pay, efficiency wage theory does not seem to provide much insight into the problem, nor much assistance to those organizations seeking to correct imbalances. Other fields offer underlying theories supporting change. Psychological theories relating to occupational choice, career counseling, and occupational segregation suggest some remedies that can be used, at least in the long run, to reduce gender-related wage differentials in any organization. Some companies, for example, are making secretarial jobs portal positions in the managerial career network along with other more traditional entry points. Others are extending career counseling and training opportunities to occupants of female-dominated jobs that have traditionally been dead ends. I do not see that efficiency wage theory offers similar support.

THE ECONOMICS OF COMPARABLE WORTH: THEORETICAL CONSIDERATIONS

Joyce P. Jacobsen

COMPENSATION of employees according to comparable worth is one of the most sweeping changes ever proposed for the U.S. economy. Its advocates argue for nothing less than a complete overhauling of the manner in which pay is determined by firms and governments. Even if only some sectors of the economy institute comparable worth policies, these limited programs could have wide-ranging effects on wages, employment, labor force participation, production, and income distribution. Comparable worth has a compelling sound of fairness, and therefore political acceptability, which, even without an economywide federal mandate, may lead to its widespread adoption through an accretion of court cases, state-level lobbying, and collective bargaining agreements. Consequently, a greater awareness of what comparable worth entails and of the arguments for and against it is needed if one is to make an educated assessment of the desirability of instituting comparable worth programs.

This paper is an attempt to contribute to the debate by synthesizing the current set of theoretical writings on comparable worth. To facilitate this exercise, I briefly survey the relevant literature, outline a particular comparable worth policy, and then lay out an economic model, namely the neoclassical perfect competition paradigm, which leads one to argue for noninterference in the labor market. I discuss the value of incorporating discrimination, imperfect competition, heterogeneous tastes, and nonindividualistic behavior into this model. My conclusion is that even when one tries to strengthen the

Helpful comments on earlier drafts of this paper from Perry Beider, David Bizer, Victor Fuchs, Sarah Lane, Carol Rapaport, Joshua Rosenbloom, Rebecca Slipe, and Steven Tomlinson are gratefully acknowledged.

case for comparable worth by modifying the basic neoclassical model, unrealistic assumptions need to be made for it to be clearly the most efficient policy. Following this discussion, I outline ways in which my basic formulation of a comparable worth policy might be modified. Next, I list some possible goals of such a policy and consider alternative policies that might enable these goals to be reached. I close with some considerations about equity, wherein I argue that comparable worth should not be advocated on the basis of absolute fairness.

Throughout I try to maintain a distinction between comparable worth as a criterion and comparable worth policies, which are specific proposals for applying this criterion. I define comparable worth as the premise that job characteristics should receive equal returns regardless of the job in which they are embodied or who performs the job. A comparable worth policy is an attempt to impose this criterion in some form in a compensation-setting environment. In that some writers use the term *comparable worth* to refer directly to a policy, the distinction has become blurred. It is a useful distinction, however, in the context of this paper.

Status of the Literature

Comparable worth has been debated extensively during the 1980s, yet the synonymic catch phrases *equal pay for equal work* and *pay equity* were heard much earlier. In the mid-1940s, comparable worth was debated when various national equal pay acts were proposed and rejected (Aldrich and Buchele 1986, 24). It was discussed again during the debates over formulation and passage of the Equal Pay Act (EPA) in 1963 (Johansen 1984, 43) but was not explicitly included in the EPA.[1] In the 1960s and 1970s some states passed comparable worth laws that covered state employees, but, much as with earlier state laws (passed in the 1940s and 1950s), these statutes were generally unenforced (Ehrenberg and Smith 1987a, 244). In 1977, comparable worth again came to national attention as a Carter administration platform (Roback 1986, 11). The National Organization for Women (NOW) and other women's rights organizations endorsed it, as did the major unions, especially those involved in organizing public employees.

In 1978 the National Committee on Pay Equity was formed; its 1981 report (Treiman and Hartmann 1981) was the first major piece

---

1. Cases have been brought under the EPA since then that argue for its applicability in such situations (Fogel 1984).

of analysis devoted to comparable worth.[2] Until this report, much of the writing on comparable worth was by lawyers and was rhetorical rather than analytical. In the 1980s, however, social scientists have written several articles and monographs on the subject. The first and easiest objective for these writers was to separate out and derogate those advocates of comparable worth who were arguing for "just pricing" of labor. The just pricing argument was usually illustrated by some unjust-sounding fact, such as that the nurses hired by the city of Denver received less on an hourly wage basis than the city's tree trimmers (Barrett 1984, 32). Such arguments were inviting targets for any economist who had learned the marginal versus absolute value paradox on Adam Smith's knee. June O'Neill (1984, 263) writes, for example:

> At least as far back as the Middle Ages, the concept of "just price" has had some appeal. Practical considerations, however, have won out over philosophical musings. Most people recognize how inefficient it would be to use an evaluation system independent of the market to set wages or prices of consumer goods. So, for example, we accept a higher price for diamonds than for water, even though water is undoubtedly more important to our survival, and a higher wage for lawyers or engineers than for clergymen or bricklayers even though they may be equally important to our well-being.

That point resolved, opponents of comparable worth next had to deal with advocates who were making the more persuasive argument that the current wage structure needs correction for inequities and distortions caused by sex discrimination; and that imposing a comparable worth policy is both a feasible and a preferable way in which to make a correction for this discrimination. In response to this line of thinking, theoretical writing and debate on comparable worth has proceeded along two tracks: how to determine equal worth and how to gauge the effects of a comparable worth policy.

The first set of papers explore the difficulties of deciding what job comparability is. These studies focus on the nuts and bolts of how jobs might be rated and the problems involved in job evaluation and classification (Treiman 1979), including innate sex-related biases (McArthur 1985), lack of agreement among evaluators as to job ratings

---

2. I can find no references to the subject before 1981, save the state of Washington's 1974 study of its job classifications, undertaken to look at male- versus female-dominated jobs (Ehrenberg and Smith 1987a, 258). The general topic of job evaluation was popular in the 1970s (see Treiman 1979 for references).

(Schwab 1985), and argument over which job factors should be compensated (Jaussad 1984). The essential question running through this line of research is whether or not one agrees with the view that "job evaluation is inherently subjective" (Aaron and Lougy 1986, 4). Opponents of comparable worth would agree with this statement and therefore argue that there is no reason to supersede the market system, given that no alternative wage system can be proven to be objectively better. Proponents of comparable worth would argue that the existing market system cannot be defended on objective grounds either, in that it allows the perpetuation of discrimination, which is taken to be objectively bad, and therefore it should carry no precedence over any other wage-setting system.[3] Because the neoclassically trained economist has already fallen back on the corollary of O'Neill's above point—"the only reliable indicator of the value of a job is the wage an employer is willing to pay a person to fill it" (Aaron and Lougy 1986, 4)—it is not surprising that they tend to opt out of the debate over how to refine job evaluation.

Nevertheless, one analytical advance in this area that has tended to draw economists back into the fray is the drawing of a distinction between "a priori" and "policy-capturing" approaches to job evaluation (Steinberg and Haignere 1984, 24–26). The former involves using point systems that assign predetermined values to skills and then rating jobs based on the sum of the point values attached to the amounts of each skill the jobs require. The latter approach involves conducting a statistical analysis (multiple regression) of the jobs in a firm based on their characteristics, adjusted for the percentage of workers in the job who are female (i.e., by formulating a hedonic equation to determine the values of skills).[4] This latter methodology has become favored over the former, as the former suffers from its "resistance to modification, general lack of flexibility or responsiveness to firm-specific factors, and probable [sex] bias" (Steinberg and

---

3. Comparable worth advocates do not present such reasoning as a proposal that the labor market system should be completely replaced by wage setting; few advocates are so impolitic as to sound as if they are proposing out-and-out government wage setting. For instance, Joy Ann Grune, perhaps the most fervent advocate of comparable worth, writes that "conceptualizing pay equity or equal pay for work of comparable value as a necessary substitute for, or as an alternative to market-based wage determination, is a partial and inaccurate way of characterizing that issue. . . . we are not saying that market-based wage setting has to be eliminated, but rather that discrimination and bias must be eliminated regardless of their sources" (1984, 5).

4. Aldrich and Buchele (1986, chap. 4) offer the most sophisticated discussion of the policy-capturing method, advocating the use of the percentage of females in an occupation as the basis for the femaleness correction factor.

Haignere 1984, 25). Both methods still suffer from the arbitrariness inherent in deciding which job characteristics should be included in the analysis.

The second line of theoretical work involves setting up a model of the economy and determining the probable effects of comparable worth within a particular framework. Using standard neoclassical theory, opponents of comparable worth attack on two grounds: a comparable worth policy would be an intolerably inefficient policy, and such a policy actually hurts some of those it is meant to help by reducing employment in jobs dominated by females. Those proponents of comparable worth who are willing to argue within the same framework counter by arguing that in fact an existing inefficiency—discrimination—will be corrected and that employment displacement will be negligibly low.

A leap to the level of estimating such a model to evaluate these conflicting claims requires that the job classification difficulties be resolved and that explicit assumptions be made about why women and men appear in occupations in different proportions (as well as a host of other technical assumptions). The most advanced effort to date is the study by Perry Beider et al. (1988), who formulated and calibrated a computable general equilibrium model. Here only two broad job classes, high skill and low skill (based on median educational attainment in an occupation), were used.

The missing element in the modeling debate has been contributions from those with a cohesive alternative view of how labor markets work. The rubric under which most dissenting work falls is the "institutional" view (Aaron and Lougy 1986, 2). Loosely, the idea here is that other variables besides labor supply and demand, such as internal job ladders and traditions about what is appropriate work for women, play a role in the setting of wages. It appears that much of what can be characterized as the feminist viewpoint on comparable worth is effectively described as institutionalist (i.e., neoclassical market models are at worst irrelevant and at best do not capture the essence of what goes on in the labor-sorting process). An alternative viewpoint to the static institutionalist framework, and one that would be compatible with much general feminist thought, is that a key outcome of comparable worth is a modification of preferences. This approach could provide a satisfactory theoretical viewpoint for countering the neoclassical model, in which tastes are exogenous. Such an alternative model would not necessarily lead to the conclusion, however, that a comparable worth policy should be adopted.

The incongruence of opposing arguments has resulted in a discourse consisting of two veins of debate: reasoning within the neoclassical framework and taking the neoclassical model to task without proposing a well-thought-through alternative. Given that the first vein dominates the second in the quantity of papers and coherence of its argument, the next section of this paper is devoted to a discussion of the neoclassical model, including the theoretical contributions made in embellishing the basic economists' model and how each alteration modifies one's conclusions about the effects of comparable worth policies.

The Perfect Competition Model and Its Extensions

A Basic Comparable Worth Policy.   For the duration of this section, let the comparable worth policy under discussion be one in which wages are raised for all holders of a job that is found under some chosen rating system to have the equivalent job points as another higher-paying job. In theory, this criterion does not need to have anything to do with the maleness or femaleness of the job (i.e., the percentage of workers in the job who are female or male). Although other policies could be implemented, such as lowering wages for some jobs or reequilibrating comparable jobs to a central point, at least in the first round of wage changes only the former strategy would be politically feasible (though downward adjustment could occur later by limiting wage increases). In this extreme case the policy would be implemented across the entire economy immediately, simultaneously, and without exception. Finally, let us assume that the policy has no transaction costs (i.e., bureaucratic and regulatory costs are nonexistent) and that firms and workers experience no adjustment costs. What effects would this comparable worth policy have on an economy?

A Basic Model.   Let us start with the case of an economy for which five blanket assumptions hold: (1) Differences in productivity across individuals are attributable to different investments in human capital; (2) all individuals are completely nondiscriminatory; (3) all industries are perfectly competitive in both factor and product markets; (4) everyone is in complete, unalterable agreement as to which job attributes are good or bad; and (5) all individuals behave atomistically; that is, family structure is irrelevant. In this model, wage differences among individuals within a job are attributable to the differing amounts of human capital embodied in those individuals; across jobs, wage differences for any given skill level are attributable to societal decisions about which jobs are more or less disagreeable. Any differences in wages and occupational distribution attributable to sex are traceable to underlying differences in productive ability. Indeed, the term *job* ceases to have much meaning here, as all work can be described using one hedonic equation in which all forms of human capital and job characteristics are entered and each person's wage rate is thereby perfectly explained. An inability on a researcher's part to explain fully any individual's wage would be attributable to insufficient or incorrectly measured data about the job and the individual's characteristics. Any attempt to realign wages in this economy would result in efficiency losses if these changes result in shifts in the distribution of factors of production or if product demand is at all sensitive to price. In this model, women would need to acquire more human capital for their wages to increase relative to those of men.

Discrimination and Collusion.   Now let us relax assumption 2 and allow discrimination to enter the model. Discrimination can lead to the "crowding" phenomenon, in which women are systematically barred from certain jobs and/or firms and are forced into the segments of the economy that are willing to hire them, albeit at a lower wage.[5] This system is hard to defend as a long-run equilibrium model because there are always profit gains to be made by nondiscriminating employers, but there are cases in which this system might be perpetuated. For instance, one could rule out the existence of nondiscriminating employers, as in Myra Strober's model, wherein all males discriminate and women do not become employers (Strober and Arnold 1987). Also, discriminating employers who are not constrained to profit-maximize by such pressures as outside stockholders can exist indefinitely.[6] In this model, an assiduous researcher who had completely accounted for individual and job characteristics

---

5. I am implicitly discussing discrimination of the type formulated first by Gary S. Becker (1971) in which employers require a wage cut to induce them to hire less desirable workers. There is a large literature both on this theory and on alternative formulations of labor market discrimination (see Cain 1986 for a recent survey), but in that most of these theories generate as outcomes segregation and/or lower wages for the discriminated-against worker class (Aldrich and Buchele 1986, chap. 3), I skip a full review of variants for lack of space.

6. In reality, discrimination may be quite pervasive, in that the quantity of anecdotal evidence from antidiscrimination cases is hard to dismiss. See Bergmann 1986 for some classic case studies.

yet still was unable to explain all of the differences between individuals' wages would be able to attribute the unexplained difference to discrimination.

If this is the case, a realignment of wages would result in much less loss of efficiency than in our first case, although the loss would still not be zero. That there would be any such loss even in this situation is an important point many comparable worth advocates overlook. Aldrich and Buchele assert, for example, that "where discrimination exists, rather than simple profit-maximizing behavior, intervention in the wage determination process can potentially improve the fairness of current labor market outcomes without reducing economic efficiency" (1986, 100). The fallacy here is in implicitly assuming that employers' tastes for discrimination are eradicated by the onset of a new wage policy. Beider et al. point out that under this system firms would still "consider women more costly than men" and that "nothing prevents a demand shift away from those jobs and sectors that are female-intensive" (1988, 32). To get a zero efficiency change, all substitution elasticities must be zero, which is a stringent assumption to make, especially for the long run.

There is another case, however, in which raising wages may improve allocative efficiency. Let us modify assumption 3 to allow for the possibility of monopsony power. If in fact all the other assumptions hold, then wage-raising intervention in the monopsonistic labor markets will be an optimal solution (Madden 1973), though not the only optimal solution. One could instead directly attack the cartels and attempt to restore the labor market to a competitive structure. Mark R. Killingsworth discusses the explicit cartelization case and concludes that "application or expansion of the antitrust laws to address such wage-fixing deserves serious consideration" (1985a, 189; see also 1985b). The plausibility of widespread monopsonistic power is questionable; if only isolated cases are found, it is difficult to see why imposition of a comparable worth policy economywide would be necessary to counteract them.

Heterogeneous Tastes.   Now let us modify assumption 4, that tastes are homogeneous, and include sex-linked differences in tastes in our model. There is a large and interesting literature on the existence of systematic differences between men and women both in what they like about work (Ferber and Spaeth 1984; Filer 1985) and in what they expect from it (Agassi 1982; Corcoran and Courant 1985; Sorensen 1984). Assume that women and men have completely different preferences for job attributes but that all men share the same preferences, as do all women. Then we would expect men and women to have nonidentical distributions across job types but would be able to say little about what the relative wages or actual distributions would be, in that they would depend on the relative supplies of male and female labor and demands for different jobs.

When one expands this case to the more general case of heterogeneous preferences, in which both men and women are distributed along continua of tastes for certain job characteristics, the theory of compensating differentials breaks down (Killingsworth 1985a, 1987). Because people now disagree about what are desirable job characteristics, there is no reason to expect that job characteristics will in fact have any discernible relation to wages. In the case in which assumption 2, the nonexistence of discrimination, is violated as well, the simple hedonic wage equation system breaks down and a researcher is now unable to say whether the unexplained portion in the regressions is attributable to job characteristics or to discrimination. Here it is unclear whether a comparable worth policy would lead to a smaller loss of efficiency than in the case in which the entire portion corrected for is attributable to discrimination—the relative result depends on the sizes of the various labor supply and demand responses.

Other Modifications of the Basic Model.   There are numerous other ways in which the basic model can be modified. Modification of assumption 3 to allow for product market power, with or without monopsony power, means that we find ourselves in a world of the "second best" where policies that lead to optimal allocative efficiency in the perfectly competitive world need not be optimal now. Unions can complicate the picture further by severing the link between personal productivity characteristics and wages and by introducing bargaining into wage determination. Allowance of the concept of efficiency wages modifies assumption 1 by making productivity dependent on pay. Aldrich and Buchele briefly mention this possibility as a way to counteract employment loss under a comparable worth policy "if the wage increase itself caused a sufficiently large increase in labor productivity so that labor costs . . . and hence employment, remained unaffected" (1986, 156).

Finally, without modifying assumption 5 somewhat, it is impossible to calculate the actual utility gains and losses of various economic players if they are making decisions in a joint-decision framework such as marriage (Beider et al. are the only writers to discuss this point). One can of course continue to assume atomistic behavior even in marriages, but a more likely case takes into account that labor market participation is altered and that income sharing within a marriage may be dependent on who makes how much.

How much do all the possible departures from the basic model matter? In the paradigmatic model, interfering with wages is undesirable on efficiency grounds; in departures from the model, a trade off exists between efficiency and equity, and one must decide both what the dimensions of the trade off are and whether or not the trade off is acceptable. It is therefore unsatisfactory to argue on theoretical grounds alone that one should either accept or reject a comparable worth policy, for the real world does not fit neatly into any simple theoretical framework. The role of theoretical discourse is rather to point out the issues to be considered in a policy debate.

Modifications of the Basic Policy.   In this section I consider in turn four modifications of the comparable worth policy discussed above: (1) the existence of an uncovered sector; (2) the realignment of wages within but not between firms; (3) the specification of a dynamic policy; and (4) nonzero implementation costs.

How might the case in which covered and uncovered sectors exist be different from the case in which there is total coverage? This is an interesting question in that the most likely development concerning comparable worth is its widespread acceptance by government bodies. In the federal case Ronald G. Ehrenberg and Robert S. Smith discuss (1987a), it is assumed that the government converts while the private sector does not. Beider et al. consider the case in which part of the private sector converts along with the government. In the latter model, labor flows out of the covered sector into the uncovered sector. Indeed, even in systems in which all wages in the formal work sector are under a comparable worth agreement, one might expect underground and home-production economies to increase in size. Beider et al. do find this in their version of the model in which the wage gap is fully attributable to discrimination; "the efficiency losses are greater than they would be with full coverage" (1988, 50).

An important consideration in these models is how to characterize the government budget constraint. Employment need not drop at all in the government sector, but in this case the whole economy would have to shrink to cover the increased government wage bill through increased taxes. If there is a binding constraint on taxes, one would expect to see an immediate reduction in employment and eventually downward adjustment of wages in the government sector (Megdal 1986). Ehrenberg and Smith conclude that employment both in female-dominated occupations within the public sector and in the public sector as a whole is likely to drop, assuming any binding budget constraint and any possibilities for substitution between labor types within the sector.

Another case is the situation in which wages are only realigned within firms (Johnson and Solon 1986). Here it is especially important to model explicitly the dynamics of the situation. One might well find that some firms have fewer job categories over time. Any firm that hires both clerks and truck drivers, for example, might contract out most of its clerical work to avoid having to pay the clerical workers the same amount as the drivers. George Johnson and Gary Solon, in their analysis of this case, decide that this is similar to the partial coverage case in that the effect of reducing the wage gap would be diminished. They make the argument that correcting only intrafirm differentials would be ineffective because it would lead to further segregation and allow male-female wage differentials to continue. Although Johnson and Solon claim this analysis is justified based on the nature of the proposals currently debated in the United States, it is unsatisfactory to dismiss comparable worth based on how one believes it will be implemented. It is not inconceivable that an economy-wide policy could be put into effect.

Perhaps the most important dimension of any proposed comparable worth scheme is the dynamics of the policy as the system goes through adjustment phases. To address this issue formally, one would need to model explicitly the reactions of the economy over time. For labor markets to clear, real wages would need to fall. In the longer run, technological change and differing capital stock would lead to the need for periodic reevaluations of the values to be attached to different job skills, in that productivity is dependent on labor's combining with varying amounts of capital and other inputs in a production process. Administrators would need to update and adapt a comparable worth policy to changing labor market conditions.

Another dynamic consideration is what hiring rules will be formulated to accompany the wage changes. Beider et al. (1988) point out that hiring rules have a major effect on how people move across occupations after a comparable worth policy is enacted. Also, just as advocates of affirmative action do not press for its being continued unchanged forever, comparable worth proposals must define the future of comparable worth explicitly, including the possibility of its being phased out.

Finally, the implementation problems and potential costs involved in setting up and administering any comparable worth policy are numerous and substantial. It is hard to debate the particulars unless one knows how close to the extreme case the policy will come, how much of the economy it will cover, how detailed the job descriptions will be, how much allowance will be built in for considerations of individual firms, what hiring rules will be enforced, and so on. In any event, the costs of implementing a comparable worth policy on any level whatsoever, including those of establishing job classifications, prosecuting wrongdoers, and handling exceptions, as well as of updating rankings and dealing with new jobs, are as yet unknown.

Conclusions

Need for a Policy.   Where does the preceding discussion of modeling lead? If differences in wages between men and women are due to differences in productivity or tastes, then no interference in the operation of the labor market is required. Rather, if one wishes to see improvement in women's incomes without direct subsidy, it should be undertaken either by improving their productivity or by changing their tastes. Almost all members of society would agree, however, that if wage differences are due to sex discrimination, coming about either because of crowding or because of systematic underpaying of women made easier through segregation (so as to get around antidiscrimination laws), these differences should be eradicated. In this case, some action needs to be taken.

Alternatives to Comparable Worth.   Comparable worth policies should not be considered in a vacuum. There are alternative policies that could meet the goals often cited in discussions of comparable worth: higher wages for women, reduced job segregation, and higher wages in occupations in which women predominate. Two commonly mentioned alternatives are increased enforcement of antidiscrimination laws and, similarly, more active affirmative action. Daniel R. Fischel and Edward P. Lazear (1986), taking their lead from antitrust theory, argue that the appropriate response to discrimination is to attack the barriers to entry for certain occupations that are the source of the inefficiency in the economy, rather than raise wages in those occupations with free entry.[7] They argue that using a comparable worth policy to attack discrimination "is analogous to attacking a

---

7. Fischel and Lazear are not the first to describe the problem as one of barriers to entry; others who formulate the problem thus include Rita Ricardo-Campbell (1985) and June O'Neill (1984). Fischel and Lazear make the argument most formally, however, and draw the analogy with product market competition.

cartel of oil producers (which results in an increase in the price of coal as consumers shift to substitute energy sources) by requiring coal producers to lower their prices" (903–4). This analogy is somewhat misleading because it assumes a profit-maximizing motive for discrimination against a group. One could, however, substitute prejudice as a motive and the argument would still be persuasive. Continuing their line of argument, any policy that attempts to lower entry barriers directly, including the two mentioned above, is preferable to a comparable worth policy.

This does not exhaust the list of alternatives. Another possibility is to transfer income directly from men to some or all women.[8] A novel idea proposed by Nancy Barrett is to give "firms that do raise pay for disadvantaged occupations . . . special tax incentives or tax credits for capital equipment that will raise the productivity of these workers" (1984, 32).

Finally, there are two extensions of the basic goal that a comparable worth policy is expected to attain, namely, that of raising women's pay relative to that of men. One may still care more about certain groups of women and wish to target them directly. One policy goal is to recompense older women who are victims of past discrimination and who lack the ability to change jobs. Then any policy that raised their income would be useful. If one rules out both subsidization of retraining and direct-income transfer, the remaining choice is to change these women's wages. If the wages are low because of overcrowding, then any policy that alleviated the overcrowding would be helpful. A comparable worth policy does not alleviate overcrowding, but it does raise wages. Vigorous enforcement of antidiscrimination statutes and affirmative action hiring, however, will channel younger women into occupations traditionally dominated by men, thereby lowering the supply of labor to the overcrowded occupations and raising the wages higher than they would otherwise be.[9] Removing the barriers to entry thus appears to be the better policy if one wants to attack overcrowding directly.

Another goal may be to raise the income levels of women and their families, especially of those women who are heads of families. Certainly poverty, especially among households headed by women with

8. Fischel and Lazear appear to be the originators of this argument and are the only writers to entertain it seriously, especially regarding the transfer of money to victims of past discrimination (1986, 909–10).

9. Johnson and Solon (1986, 1119) feel that this would not affect the wages of older women but provide no support for their position—one would presumably have to argue that older workers in a given job are imperfect substitutes for younger labor.

dependents, is a pressing issue. Under comparable worth, some families and individuals are hurt and some are helped. Again, it is hard to see why this is a better policy for raising low incomes than transferring income directly or providing better access to higher-paying jobs in male-dominated fields. In this case, it becomes crucial to model whether the expected response to a policy is a decline in employment or in the hours each employee works. Job sharing would push fewer people below the poverty line.

Final Considerations. James L. Medoff recently wrote that "to me, comparable worth is much more an issue of fairness and implementation than one of economic efficiency, since I would not favor discriminating against any demographic group, even if such discrimination significantly increased national income" (1987, 289). While I agree with the emphasis on implementation (i.e., the bringing to earth of discussions of comparable worth to specifics of certain policies), I find reliance on universal understanding of discrimination and fairness to be misguided.

How are worthy groups defined, and should we define groups for policy purposes at all? Another economist, Lester C. Thurow, has written that "every society has to have a theory of legitimate and illegitimate groups, when individuals can be judged on group data and when they cannot be judged on group data" (1979, 173). Under this line of thought, such a theory is therefore societally specific rather than universal. Thurow suggests two criteria for whether or not a group can legitimately claim compensation based on having been disadvantaged: whether mobility out of the group is possible and whether members of the group can claim they have been handicapped by past discrimination. By these criteria, affirmative action, for example, appears to be a defensible policy.

Any compensation scheme is still defensible only to the extent that society considers it to be recompense for a legitimate complaint, rather than on absolute grounds of fairness, for one can argue that discrimination on any grounds by a group rather than by an individual is fundamentally unfair (Thurow 1979, 171). This argument clearly applies to discrimination in favor of a group as well, for even correcting a past wrong will involve some disadvantaging of those not covered. Yet, unless there is a one-to-one match between job types and individuals, comparable worth policies will treat like people unequally and different people equally. There is no reason to assume that two people filling the same job are equally productive. Better to provide an environment in which people can find their best niches on their own rather than decide in some nonconsensual way what characteristics are and are not compensable.

Finally, any decision about what is a compensable characteristic may be fundamentally unfair from an income distribution point of view, whether the market or the government sets the wage scales. If the concern is income distribution, it is not even absolutely defensible to reward persons based on their own productivity. As Robert Nozick points out, all societies make fundamental assumptions about which human traits a person is allowed to hold title to (1974, cf. chap. 7 on distributive justice). In our society, we allow genetic gifts to be held as human capital and allow wealth to be passed from generation to generation (albeit with some run-off through income and inheritance taxation). Fairness is ultimately a relative concept—we set the rules for the market as to what may be traded and what may be kept. In this sense, American society may need to renegotiate its social contract in a more fundamental way than supporters of comparable worth can currently see fit to advocate. This renegotiation may be more wide ranging than comparable worth, or more narrow. In either case, such a renegotiation is ultimately outside the realm of economics and instead within the realm of politics, and its course cannot be predicted by the social sciences as they now stand.

DISCUSSION

Rebecca M. Blank

Joyce Jacobsen has provided a useful review of many of the major issues in the comparable worth debate. Her main goal is to critique the theoretical arguments for and against comparable worth from the perspective of neoclassical economics, which she does quite succinctly. Her discussion of the extent to which a standard neoclassical model might support a comparable worth policy if modifications were made to the typical competitive market assumptions is particularly useful. There are three areas of her discussion, however, on which I would like to expand.

First, by underemphasizing the problems involved in using administratively determined wage-setting regimes, Jacobsen has been less critical of comparable worth than many neoclassical economists would be. The presumption in neoclassical models is that any intervention that removes wages from the competitive auction market environment is undesirable. Comparable worth policies that mandate particular wage scales or wage relationships across jobs implement a wage system that may not be responsive to market forces.

Jacobsen notes that if discrimination is present in the market, a "realignment of wages would result in much less of a loss in efficiency." (The loss would still be nonzero because of shifts away from occupations and industries in which employers still wish to discriminate.) This movement toward greater efficiency will occur, however, only if wages are realigned closer to the competitive (nondiscriminatory) market price and are then allowed to change over time as market forces change. To the extent that comparable worth involves the imposition of a more rigid wage scale (and regardless of how "comparability" is computed, recomputations will be expensive and thus infrequent) there is no guarantee that the readjustment comparable worth would bring about would result in a new wage scale that was permanently closer to the competitive equilibrium. Thus, even in cases in which discrimination or other forms of market failure were creating market distortions, a comparable worth policy might not be an attractive remedy.

Second, Jacobsen fails to mention one of the primary problems in the manner by which standard economic models describe discrimination. Assume a comparable worth policy is proposed to eliminate the effects of discrimination in the labor market. As Jacobsen notes, if the preference or taste for discrimination on the part of employers is not affected by the policy, inefficiencies will result from the implementation of comparable worth, as firms shift employment away from jobs and industries in which women are likely to seek employment. This raises the critical issue of how these discriminatory tastes are perpetuated or reduced, an area on which economic theories of discrimination have been largely silent.

Economists have traditionally defined the issue of preference formation as outside their realm. Yet, in discussing the impact of comparable worth, potential changes in the taste for discrimination are critically important. The crucial question is, Will changes in behavior (forced by legislation) induce changes in attitude? If forcing employers to change their behavior and hire women at a higher wage induces them to rethink their previous discriminatory impulses, then a short-term realignment of wages may induce long-term behavioral change, leading to a long-run decrease in discrimination that will offset any inefficiencies involved in implementing comparable worth. To assume that antidiscrimination policies do not change the taste for discrimination is to discount one of the primary policy arguments for antidiscrimination measures. The inability of economic models to deal with such potential changes in the nature of discriminatory behavior makes them less useful in evaluating antidiscrimination policies such as comparable worth.

Third, and finally, the question raised at the end of Jacobsen's article is an important one: given that comparable worth involves certain costs, are there other ways to achieve similar objectives (i.e., the breakdown of gender-based discrimination) that may be less costly or more attractive to neoclassical economists? I think Jacobsen overstates the attraction of affirmative action laws here and ignores an important alternative.

Affirmative action laws in this country are quite limited with respect to the discrimination they address. They apply to wage levels and hiring within similar job categories. The whole point of the comparable worth debate is to indicate that equal pay for equal jobs is not enough. Thus, if the claims of the proponents of comparable worth are correct and discrimination influences the relative wage levels paid to whole sets of more predominantly female occupations and industries (as evidence presented in other papers in this volume indicate), then current affirmative action and equal opportunity laws are not designed to deal with such pervasive problems. While active and ongoing enforcement of the current laws certainly will help break down barriers within job categories, it will not address the "comparability" problem of valuation.

One alternative Jacobsen does not mention is worker organization on the part of women in more predominantly female occupations and industries. Unionization is the traditional route by which groups of workers have raised wages and changed their terms of employment. In fact, the only areas in which unionization has been growing are certain service occupations and public-sector jobs, which are often dominated by women. A comparison in particular occupations of the costs and benefits of raising wages through unionization rather than through comparable worth would be interesting.

Overall, Jacobsen has provided a useful review of some of the major neoclassical responses to comparable worth proposals. Ultimately I agree with the tenor of her analysis, namely, that it is difficult to justify comparable worth within a neoclassical framework. Alternative models may provide a stronger supporting presumption for comparable worth policies, but, as Jacobsen notes, a solid theoretical argument for comparable worth out of an institutionalist paradigm does not yet exist in the literature. I agree with her that it is the political and institutional issues emphasized within this paradigm that provide the strongest arguments for a comparable worth policy.

Nonetheless, I think it is important to take seriously the economist's concern with opportunity cost on this issue. Even if a solid theoretical justification for comparable worth can be made, that does not imply that a comparable worth policy would be the most effective way to combat male-female wage differentials in the labor market. The advantages and costs of comparable worth should be discussed in comparison with the advantages and costs of alternative means to overcome low wages and labor market discrimination. Given the need to implement public policies aimed at lessening gender-based discrimination in the labor market, it is worthwhile trying to choose programs that will provide the greatest return on the effort.

Barbara A. Lee

It is a pleasure to respond to Joyce Jacobsen's paper for two reasons. First, she has provided a clear synthesis of the comparable worth debate from the neoclassical perspective in terms a lawyer untrained in economics can understand. And second, while criticizing the approach championed by proponents of comparable worth, she presents several alternative strategies which, she argues, could lead to greater wage equity and lower occupational segregation. Her willingness to propose alternatives, rather than simply criticizing the proposals of comparable worth proponents, is laudable.

Although Jacobsen offers several alternatives, she appears to favor one above the others, and my comments will focus on the one she chooses as "the better policy." The primary strategy Jacobsen suggests is one I believe has been shown to be ineffective in closing the wage gap between men and women. Jacobsen advocates "increased enforcement of antidiscrimination laws and . . . more affirmative action" as "preferable to a comparable worth policy." Neither of the two problems that advocates of pay equity seek to address—occupational segregation and crowding of women in low-paying jobs and the barriers to women seeking to enter male-dominated jobs—have been or can be effectively addressed by this strategy.

The legal system has not provided a remedy for the wage gap between male- and female-dominated jobs that results from occupational segregation and crowding. The courts have clearly rejected the notion that Title VII of the Civil Rights Act of 1964, or other antidiscrimination laws, require employers to pay women equal wages for jobs that are dissimilar but of equal "value" to the employer. The most recent and most clearly articulated rejection of this legal strategy appears in the Ninth Circuit's opinion in *AFSCME v. State of Washington* [770 F.2d 1401 (9th Cir. 1985)]. The court stated that organizations have the right to follow the market valuation of jobs, even if this results in pay gaps between men and women; unless the jobs being compared involved equal skill, effort, responsibility, and working conditions, no legal challenge to the pay allocated to the job was possible. The fact that the "market" is the aggregation of the decisions of individual employers has not been viewed by the courts as relevant to the legal analysis.

Furthermore, Jacobsen's confidence in the ability of affirmative action to remove barriers to women seeking to enter male-dominated occupations is overly optimistic. Currently, state and federal civil rights laws do not require affirmative action, and, in fact, four justices sitting on the U.S. Supreme Court read Title VII of the Civil

Rights Act of 1964 as forbidding affirmative action (*Johnson v. Transportation Agency of Santa Clara County*, 107 S. Ct. 1442 (1987)). For affirmative action to be effective in removing gender barriers, state and federal civil rights laws would have to be amended (an unlikely event given the current political climate). Identifying those jobs for which affirmative action would be required would very likely engender as much social disruption and litigation as that predicted by comparable worth opponents if comparable worth were imposed by law.

Some might argue that affirmative action is not necessary, however, because individuals who are qualified for a job but are denied employment on the basis of gender may simply challenge that decision in court. Superficially, this approach seems efficient, in that only those women who want to enter male-dominated jobs will sue, while women who prefer to remain in female-dominated occupations and are satisfied with the concomitant lower pay will not. Enforcing the anti-discrimination laws through a series of individual lawsuits, however, is neither an efficient nor an effective strategy for removing these barriers.

First, litigation is an expensive, slow process that frequently motivates plaintiffs to accept a cash settlement rather than continue a lawsuit whose purpose is to force an employer to hire them for a job from which they have been barred on gender grounds. Many attorneys insist that plaintiffs pay the litigation costs as they arise, rather than agreeing to a contingent fee arrangement, thus discouraging many women from pursuing legal challenges. Moreover, government agencies charged with enforcing the antidiscrimination laws are understaffed and press for settlement of complaints rather than representing plaintiffs with strong cases in the litigation process.

Second, those women who do go to court have found that winning a discrimination lawsuit is very difficult, and the majority of plaintiffs do not prevail. The burden of proving discrimination is heavy, and most employers can provide some "legitimate nondiscriminatory reason" for a refusal to hire or promote. Scholars have noted the deference judges give to the judgments of employers in hiring and promotion decisions, particularly when white-collar or professional jobs are at issue (Bartholet 1982; Waintroob 1979–80); these jobs are the very ones most likely to be dominated by males. Research conducted on challenges by college faculty under the federal antidiscrimination laws between 1972 and 1984 showed that only 20 percent of the plaintiffs were successful (LaNoue and Lee 1987).

Third, one might question the propriety, from a public policy perspective, of expecting the combined effect of the efforts of individual plaintiffs to result in a more equitable compensation system.

Economists might argue that, assuming rationality, the expense of defending discrimination litigation will deter employers from discriminating. The data suggest otherwise. Furthermore, the decisions of many plaintiffs to accept a modest cash settlement, combined with the low success rate of those plaintiffs who do pursue their claims in court, demonstrate that there is little economic disincentive for employers to practice discrimination.

In our society, litigation should be the last alternative for solving a social problem. In the context of the comparable worth debate, litigation is not only an inappropriate policy tool but expensive, ineffective, and inefficient. Furthermore, litigation can react to a problem only after it occurs; it cannot prevent the problem, and frequently, as in this case, it cannot solve it.

—————————— 4 ——————————

THE WAGE EFFECTS OF OCCUPATIONAL SEX COMPOSITION: A REVIEW AND NEW FINDINGS

Elaine Sorensen

ALTHOUGH the earnings of females relative to those of males have increased during the past few years, a large pay gap still exists. In 1986, full-time female workers still earned only 64 percent as much as full-time male workers, the same ratio as in 1955 (U.S. Bureau of the Census 1987a). In addition, although the degree of occupational segregation has decreased somewhat during the past two decades, it was still true in 1981 that more than 60 percent of the female (or male) labor force would have had to change jobs for the two sex groups to have the same detailed occupational distribution (Beller 1984).

Some believe that a comparable worth policy can reduce the sex-based earnings disparity. Such proponents argue that the earnings differential persists in large part because of occupational segregation, which allows firms to pay lower wages to workers in jobs with an over-representation of women or minorities. The purpose of a comparable worth policy is to eliminate the effect of occupational segregation on earnings within a firm once legitimate variables that influence earnings have been taken into account.

Others argue that occupational segregation within a firm is not a major factor contributing to the earnings disparity. Instead, a significant portion of the earnings gap is explained by differences in productivity-related characteristics (O'Neill 1983). Still others claim that differences in the industrial distribution between women and men is a major factor contributing to the persistence of the earnings gap (Johnson and Solon 1984). Thus comparable worth policies cannot effectively reduce the male-female earnings gap.

The purpose of this paper is to examine the discrimination literature that focuses on the impact of occupational segregation on earnings. Both the theoretical and empirical literature are reviewed. The theoretical literature postulates why occupational segregation reduces earnings; the empirical literature estimates the magnitude of this relationship. I find that both literatures are inconclusive. New empirical results are then presented and contrasted with existing literature. These findings are based on data from the 1984 Panel Survey of Income Dynamics.

Review of the Theoretical Literature

Two discrimination theories postulate why occupational segregation contributes to the male-female earnings gap: the crowding hypothesis and the institutional approach. Both theories have been used to justify a comparable worth policy.

According to the crowding model, employers discriminate against women by excluding them from occupations that are considered to be "men's work" (Bergmann 1986). These occupations, such as truck driving or the building trades, are reserved for men, resulting in fewer women being hired. Because the demand for women is limited in these occupations, they are crowded into other occupations, typically referred to as "women's work." The supply of women is accordingly increased for women's work, which in turn reduces their wages. This model assumes that women and men have equal abilities and that without discrimination they would be paid equally. Consequently, it predicts that, because of discrimination, women and men are segregated into different occupations and that those doing women's work earn less than those doing men's work even though they are equally productive.

An institutional model of the labor market has also been used to explain the effect of occupational segregation on the sex-based earnings differential (Doeringer and Piore 1971; Treiman and Hartmann 1981; Marshall and Paulin 1984). According to this theory, most firms develop internal labor markets, within which the pricing and allocation of labor is governed by a set of rules and customs rather than by direct supply-and-demand considerations. Management adopts internal labor markets to reduce training and turnover costs; employees prefer the arrangement because it offers increased job security and promotional opportunities. The criteria that govern the operation of internal labor markets, however, reflect societal norms and the social order within the larger community. These norms have enabled separate roles to be established and maintained for women and men and for women's work to be less valued than men's. Firms incorporate and reinforce these norms within an internal labor market by restricting women's occupational opportunities to certain occupations and by paying the women in these occupations less than they would if the jobs were performed by men, simply because women's work is less valued by society. Thus the rules governing an internal labor market reflect and reproduce societal discrimination against women.

Several implications can be drawn from these models. First, although both models assert that employer discrimination reduces the earnings of workers employed in female-dominated jobs, the process whereby wages are reduced is quite different. The crowding model posits that employer discrimination restricts women's employment opportunities to certain occupations deemed women's work. This increases the supply of workers for these jobs, and, as a result, earnings are depressed in these occupations. In contrast, the institutional model claims that employers segregate their work force and pay less in female-dominated jobs than in male-dominated jobs not because of crowding but because of custom, which has traditionally undervalued the work women do. Consequently, according to the institutional model, demand factors reduce earnings in female-dominated jobs while, according to the crowding model, supply factors contribute to lower earnings.

Second, these models posit that both male and female workers earn lower wages when they are employed in female-dominated jobs than when they are in male-dominated jobs. Under the crowding model, the earnings of men in these jobs will be lower because of the excess supply of women in these occupations. Under the institutional model, the men's earnings will be lower because wages are attached to jobs, not individuals, and thus if men are employed in female-dominated jobs, they too will suffer from its undervaluation.

Third, neither model has a complete formulation of the discrimination process. Instead, they focus on the link between occupational segregation and earnings, overlooking other aspects of discrimination. Neither model explains, for example, how occupations become dominated by either females or males. Nor do they explain why competitive pressures do not erode discrimination in the long run. Additional modeling of this process is needed to understand further the dynamics of discrimination. Nonetheless, both theories provide a description of this process that links occupational segregation with lower earnings in female-dominated jobs.

Review of the Empirical Literature

Both theories predict that, all else being equal, employment in a job held predominantly by women will reduce an individual's earnings. One way to test this hypothesis is to estimate an earnings equation that includes an independent variable that measures the proportion of workers in an occupation who are women (PF) as well as other more traditional explanatory factors. A significant coefficient for this variable would imply that the aforementioned hypothesis cannot be rejected and indicate that the gender composition of an occupation is a statistically important determinant of earnings. This result would be consistent with both theories of discrimination described above.

Several studies that examine the earnings equations of males and females have included a measure of the sex composition of an occupation as an independent variable and thus offer evidence regarding this hypothesis. A summary of the results of these studies is shown in table 4.1. Marianne A. Ferber and Helen M. Lowry (1976) were among the first to estimate separate occupational earnings equations for men and women. They used data on 260 detailed occupations from the 1970 U.S. Census. Their dependent variable was the median annual earnings of men (or women) in an occupation. Their explanatory factors were the median years of schooling of the male (or female) workers in an occupation and the proportion of workers who were male. They found that men earned an average of $5,008 less per year if they worked in an occupation that employed women almost exclusively. Women earned an average of $1,438 less per year if they were similarly employed. Unfortunately, Ferber and Lowry did not provide sufficient information to determine the extent to which this factor contributes to the overall male-female earnings differential. Consequently, this section of table 4.1 is left blank.

Paula England, Marilyn Chassie, and Linda McCormack (1982) also used 1970 Census data to estimate separate occupational earnings equations for women and men. They included 387 detailed occupations in their analysis and examined only full-time year-round workers. Their dependent variable was the median annual earnings of full-time male (or female) workers in an occupation. Their independent variables were twenty-two job characteristics, which were derived from the *Dictionary of Occupational Titles* (*DOT*), as well as the proportion of women in an occupation. They found that men earned an average of $3,005 less per year in a female-dominated occupation than in a male-dominated occupation. Women earned an average of $1,682 less per year under similar circumstances. Using data from England et al., I find that the sex composition of an occupation accounts for 21 to 38 percent of the male-female earnings gap, depending on whether the estimated coefficient used in the derivation is for females or males.[1]

June O'Neill (1983) examined the March 1980 Current Population Survey.[2] She estimated separate occupational earnings for women and men, using a sample size of 306 occupations. The dependent variables were the logarithmic hourly earnings of female and male workers in an occupation, respectively. In her analysis, she included a number of control variables, as indicated in table 4.1. She found that women earned 16 percent less when they were employed in occupations dominated completely by women than in virtually all-male occupations. Men earned 15 percent less under similar circumstances. Furthermore, in this analysis occupational segregation explains 11 to 12 percent of the male-female earnings gap, depending on whether the estimated coefficient used in the derivation is for males or females.

Mark Aldrich and Robert Buchele (1986) examined National Longitudinal Survey data for young women (ages twenty-six to thirty-six) and men (ages twenty-eight to thirty-eight) in 1980. Using a sample size of 192 occupations, they also estimated separate occupational earnings equations for women and men. They found that men earned an average of $0.69 less per hour if they were employed in jobs dominated completely by women, or $1,427 less per year, assuming a full-time year-round employee works 2,080 hours per year. Women earned an average of $0.59 less per hour, or $1,227 less per year, under similar circumstances. Using these data, I find that 9 to 11 percent of the earnings gap is explained by the variable measuring the sex composition of an occupation, depending on whether the estimated coefficient used in the derivation is for females or males.

As table 4.1 indicates, unlike other studies reviewed, these four studies used as their unit of observation occupations weighted by the

---

1. See table 4.1, n. e, for the formula to calculate the proportion of the male-female earnings gap explained by occupational segregation.

2. O'Neill also examined data from the 1978 National Longitudinal Survey of Young Women. The estimated earnings equations, however, included two measures of the sex composition of the worker's occupation, making it difficult to compare these results with the other studies in this review. The discussion here will therefore focus on O'Neill's CPS results.

Table 4.1. Summary of Studies Examining Female-Male Earnings as a Function of an Occupation's Sex Composition

Study	Source	Measure of Earnings[e]	Pay Ratio	Estimated Coefficients[a]		Percentage of Gap Explained by Sex Composition[b]			Unit of Analysis[c]	Control Variables[d]
						Coefficients		Average		
						Female	Male			
Ferber and Lowry (1976)	1970 Census	Median annual		−1438	−5008				Weighted occup. (n = 260)	1, 2
Snyder and Hudis (1979)	1970 Census	Median annual		−2070	−3900				Unweighted occup. (n = 212)	1, 2, 7, 11, 27
Treiman and Hartmann (1981)	1970 Census	Median annualized[e]		−1630	−2960				Unweighted occup. (n = 499)	1
England, et al. (1982)	1970 Census	Median annual for full-time workers	.54	−1682	−3005	21%	38%	30%	Weighted occup. (n = 387)	1, 26, 27, 29, 30, 31, 32
Aldrich and Buchele (1986)	1980 NLS	Hourly	.64	−.586	−.686	9	11	10	Weighted occup. (n = 192)	1, 2, 4, 5, 6, 7, 12, 13, 14, 26, 27, 33
O'Neill (1983)	1980 CPS	Log hourly	.68	−.158 (.049)	−.148 (.049)	12	11	11	Weighted occup. (n = 306)	1, 2, 6, 7, 11, 18, 27, 28, 36, 37, 38, 39
Johnson and Solon (1984)	1978 CPS	Log hourly	.66	−.090 (.014)	−.168 (.015)	11	21	16	Individual n_f = 19,412	1, 2, 3, 6, 7, 8, 9, 10, 12, 13, 15,

Study	Data	Dependent variable		nhs/hs/col							Sample		
U.S. Census (1987b)	1984 SIPP	Log hourly for full-time workers	.70	nhs[f]	−.340 (.067)	−.241 (.060)	43	30	37		n_m = 24,056 Individual n_f = 5,555 n_m = 8,167	26, 27, 28, 36	1, 4, 5, 7, 8, 9, 10, 12, 13, 16, 17, 18, 19, 20, 21, 22, 23, 24, 25, 34
				hs	−.211 (.033)	−.225 (.026)	28	30	29				
				col	−.417 (.061)	−.189 (.056)	38	17	28				
Sorensen	1984 PSID	Log hourly	.65		−.230 (.033)	−.239 (.040)	23	24	23		Individual n_f = 2,411 n_m = 2,616	23	1, 2, 4, 5, 6, 7, 8, 9, 10, 12, 13, 15, 19, 23, 24, 26, 27, 28, 35

[a] All measured as the proportion of workers in an occupation who are female except Aldrich and Buchele, which is percent female. Standard errors are in parentheses.

[b] Blanks exist because data were unavailable to calculate these figures or unweighted occupations were used as the unit of analysis and thus individual inferences could not be made. The percentage of the pay gap accounted for by the sex composition of an occupation using the male coefficient was calculated as follows: $b_m (X_m - X_f) / (ln\ w_m - ln\ w_f)$. X_m and X_f are the sample means of the proportion of women in an occupation for men and women, respectively. $ln\ w_m$ and $ln\ w_f$ are the sample means of log hourly earnings for men and women. b_m is the male regression coefficient for the proportion of women in an occupation. To derive the figure using the female coefficient, b_m is replaced by b_f.

[c] Weighted occup. = each observation is an occupation weighted by the proportion of the female or male work force in the occupation; unweighted occup. = each observation is an occupation; individual = each observation is an individual worker; n = the number of observations; n_f = the number of female observations; n_m = the number of male observations.

[d] Control variables are (1) sex composition of an occupation, (2) education, (3) potential work experience, (4) actual work experience, (5) tenure (job and/or employer tenure), (6) region, (7) urban, (8) race, (9) marital status, (10) children (number and/or presence), (11) hours of work, (12) union status (membership and/or coverage), (13) government employment, (14) industry dummies—core/periphery distinctions, (15) two-digit SIC code industrial categories, (16) firm size, (17) involuntarily left last job, (18) turnover, (19) health/disability, (20) blue-collar occupation, (21) high school curriculum, (22) attended private high school, (23) obtained advanced degree, (24) obtained college degree, (25) various fields of study in college, (26) general educational development (DOT), (27) specific vocational preparation (DOT), (28) DOT measures of working conditions, (29) DOT measures of cognitive skills, (30) DOT measures of perceptual skills, (31) DOT measures of manual skills, (32) DOT measures of social skills, (33) race composition of an occupation, (34) usually work full time, (35) part time last year, (36) part time this year, (37) employed five years earlier, (38) license or certification required, and (39) self-employed.

[e] Median annualized earnings = (median annual earnings * 2,080)/mean annual hours.

[f] nhs = not a high school graduate; hs = high school graduate; col = college graduate.

proportion of male or female workers in each. Consequently, these authors make inferences about individuals but used aggregated units of analysis. Unfortunately, aggregation inevitably results in less efficient estimation and may lead to aggregation bias. Because these studies analyzed individual behavior, using individuals as the unit of observation would offer a more appropriate analytic design.

Alternatively, occupations could be used as the unit of analysis without weighting them by the proportion of women or men employed in the occupation. This approach tests a different hypothosis, however: that occupational segregation reduces earnings in an occupation rather than those of individuals. The studies by David Snyder and Paula M. Hudis (1979) and by Donald J. Treiman and Heidi I. Hartmann (1981) take this approach.

Snyder and Hudis and Treiman and Hartmann estimated separate occupational earnings equations for women and men using 1970 Census data without weighting each occupation by the proportion of women and men employed in it. (Snyder and Hudis used 212 occupations in their analysis; Treiman and Hartmann used 499.) Snyder and Hudis used median annual earnings as their dependent variable and a variety of independent factors, including the median education of workers in the occupation and the percentage of workers who work a full week and the percentage who work a full year. They found that men are paid $3,900 less per year in jobs dominated completely by women than in jobs dominated by men. Women are paid $2,070 less per year in similar circumstances.

Treiman and Hartmann used median "annualized" earnings as the dependent variable (i.e., they multiplied median annual earnings in an occupation by 2,080, the estimated annual hours worked by full-time year-round workers, and divided by the actual annual hours worked on average in that occupation). The only independent factor in their analysis was the percentage of women in an occupation. They found that the earnings difference for men between female-dominated and male-dominated jobs was $2,960 per year. The earnings difference for women was $1,630 per year.

Because these studies analyze occupations rather than individuals, inferences cannot be made about individuals. This is an unfortunate drawback of this analytic design, especially because discrimination is usually conceived as affecting individuals rather than occupations. Because of this limitation, these studies cannot be used to determine the percentage of the male-female earnings gap due to the sex composition of an occupation. Thus this section of table 4.1 is left blank.

All six of the studies that use occupations rather than individuals as their unit of observation, especially those using the 1970 Census data, employ relatively few control variables in their analyses. Omitting such variables, which are known to affect earnings and may be correlated with the sex composition of an occupation, will bias the estimated effect of occupational segregation on earnings. Ferber and Lowry, for example, examine annual earnings without controlling for differences in hours worked between women and men. Clearly, hours worked increases annual earnings and may be positively correlated with the proportion of men in an occupation, a variable Ferber and Lowry use in their analysis. Consequently, omitting hours worked will cause the estimated coefficient for the proportion of men in an occupation to overestimate the true effect of this variable on earnings. Treiman and Hartmann account for male-female differences in hours worked by examining annualized earnings, but they do not control for any other factor known to affect earnings other than the sex composition of an occupation. Variables such as education or occupational characteristics are undoubtedly correlated with the sex composition of the occupation. Omitting these variables thus yields a biased estimate of the effect of occupational segregation on earnings.

The studies by Snyder and Hudis and by England et al. go beyond the work of Ferber and Lowry and Treiman and Hartmann by controlling for hours worked and occupational characteristics, but these studies do not account for individual differences between women and men. None of these studies accounts for sex differences in actual or potential work experience, for example. These factors increase earnings and probably are correlated with the sex composition of an occupation. Thus, omitting them from the analysis will also result in a biased estimate of the effect of occupational segregation on earnings. In principle, a causal effect between occupational segregation and earnings would be demonstrated net all other possible influences on the dependent variable. Any known determinant of earnings should therefore be included in the analysis.

The studies by O'Neill and by Aldrich and Buchele also include considerably more control variables in their analyses than the aforementioned studies; however, both of these studies have other serious problems that vitiate their results. O'Neill estimates earnings equations separately for women and men, for example, but, except for the variable measuring work experience, she does not measure control variables separately for women and men. Women and men employed in the same occupation will thus have the same rates of occupational turnover and education even though the women and men in the occupation most likely have different rates. Consequently, O'Neill analyzes the earnings behavior of women and men as a function of the average characteristics of individuals in their occupation. The more typical approach, motivated by human capital theory, is to examine the earnings behavior of women (or men) as a function of the characteristics of women (or men). An alternative approach, discussed above, is to analyze occupational earnings as a function of occupational characteristics. Unfortunately, O'Neill mixed these two analytic designs without any explanation.

The work by Aldrich and Buchele avoids the drawbacks of O'Neill's work by measuring control variables separately for women and men, except for those variables that are characteristics of the occupation, such as the sex composition. Their analysis has other problems, however, that are equally troubling. First, they measure the critical variable, the proportion of women in an occupation, using a sample size of only 3,297 individuals, which averages to only 17 individuals per occupation. These figures are insufficient for estimating a reliable measure of the proportion of women in an occupation. Thus they measure the sex composition of an occupation with error. This potential measurement error may bias the ordinary least squares estimated coefficient for this variable toward zero. Second, Aldrich and Buchele use the 1960 Census occupational categories, which have been heavily criticized for their extensive use of broad categories referred to as "not elsewhere classified" (n.e.c.). In 1960, five of these categories (n.e.c. for professional, clerical, sales, operatives, and laborers) included more than 20 percent of the total labor force. These five categories were subsequently divided into more than fifty occupations in the 1970 Census. Aldrich and Buchele apparently used all five of these categories in their analysis. Such broad occupational categories disguise part of the negative relationship between occupational segregation and earnings. Including them in an analysis will thus tend to reduce the magnitude of this negative relationship.

The last two studies, conducted by Johnson and Solon (1984) and by the U.S. Bureau of the Census (1987b), are quite similar in certain ways. Both studies used individuals as the unit of analysis, which, as stated earlier, provides a more appropriate framework for analyzing the effect of occupational segregation on individual earnings. Both studies used the proportion of women in an occupation as an independent variable, and both used logarithmic hourly earnings as the dependent variable. Finally, both studies derived the proportion of women in an occupation from annual Current Population Survey (CPS) data.

Despite these similarities, there are two major differences between these studies. First, Johnson and Solon used May 1978 CPS data on 24,056 men and 19,412 women. In contrast, the Census Bureau used 1984 Survey of Income and Program Participation (SIPP) data on 8,167 full-time male workers and 5,555 full-time female workers. More important, the set of control variables contrast sharply between these two studies. Johnson and Solon, for example, included detailed industry control variables while the Census Bureau did not. Because women are segregated by industry as well as by occupation, it is useful to measure these influences on earnings separately. It is then possible to estimate the relative contribution of industrial and occupational segregation to the male-female earnings disparity. In addition, because comparable worth policies are designed to eliminate the effect of occupational segregation within firms, any negative impact that industrial segregation may have on earnings will be unaffected by comparable worth policies. Consequently, for policy purposes it would be useful to estimate these two influences on earnings separately. These considerations led Johnson and Solon to include twenty industry dummy variables in their analysis.

The data employed by the Census Bureau have much richer measures of work experience and education than the CPS data used by Johnson and Solon. Thus the Census Bureau included measures of actual work experience, job tenure, education, whether an advanced degree was completed, and the field of study while in college. Johnson and Solon included only education and potential work experience. Of course, a model of the relationship between occupational segregation and individual earnings should include accurate measures of both human capital and industry control variables. Such a design would enable one to estimate separately the impact of all three variables on earnings. Unfortunately, neither of these studies includes such variables.

The differences in control variables are the principal reason these studies have such opposite results. On the one hand, Johnson and Solon found that women earn only 9 percent less in occupations that hire women almost exclusively than in those that hire mostly men. They found that men in these circumstances earn 17 percent less.[3]

---

3. Johnson and Solon (1984) report a number of different estimates for the effect on earnings of being employed in a female-dominated occupation. The smallest estimates occur when they include forty-eight industry dummies. These figures are 7 percent less for women and 16 percent less for men, instead of the 9 percent and 17 percent I report in the text. My figures are based on the regressions with only twenty industry dummies, which are the regression results Johnson and Solon used to decompose the

The sex composition of an occupation explains only 11 to 21 percent of the male-female earnings differential, depending on whether the coefficient used in the derivation is for males or females. On the other hand, the Census Bureau found that women who have not graduated from high school earn an average of 34 percent less if they are employed in virtually all-female jobs rather than virtually all-male jobs. Men in similar circumstances earn 24 percent less. Thus 30 to 43 percent of this earnings gap is explained by the sex composition of an occupation. The findings are somewhat less significant for workers who have completed high school, but the effects are still almost twice as large as those found by Johnson and Solon.

In summary, all of the studies report a significant coefficient for the variable measuring the sex composition of an occupation, indicating that employment in a female-dominated job reduces earnings. The magnitude of this effect varies considerably, however. Occupational segregation accounts for anywhere from 10 to 30 percent of the sex-based earnings gap. In addition, existing empirical research is hindered by two fundamental drawbacks. First, most studies use occupations (weighted by the proportion of male or female workers employed in the occupation) as their unit of analysis rather than individuals. Unfortunately, this aggregation results in less efficient estimation and possible aggregation bias, without any apparent gain. Second, most of the studies omit detailed industry control variables, and thus the effect of occupational segregation and the impact of the differing industrial distributions of women and men on earnings cannot be separated. The only study that overcomes both of these fundamental drawbacks used a data set that had only weak measures of human capital variables (Johnson and Solon 1984). Insofar as these findings strongly suggest that additional research is needed, a study was undertaken using data from the 1984 Panel Study of Income Dynamics (PSID), which eliminates the shortcomings described above.

Discussion of the Data

Separate earnings equations were estimated for women and men using data from the 1984 PSID. The data consisted of all heads of households and wives of at least eighteen years old who reported their hourly earnings. For the reasons outlined above, individuals

---

influence of the control variables and which I examine more closely later in this paper. I report these figures throughout to avoid any confusion.

were selected as the unit of analysis. The dependent variable was the natural logarithm of hourly earnings. This variable averaged 2.313 for the men in this sample and 1.890 for the women; the difference was 0.423. The ratio of the mean wages of females to the mean wages for males was 0.65. There were 2,616 men in the sample and 2,411 women.

The independent variable measuring the proportion of women in an occupation was constructed from a 20 percent sample from the 1980 U.S. Census (1983), which includes 503 occupational categories taken from the three-digit Standard Occupational Classification (SOC) system. The PSID data, however, used 1970 Census data, which have 499 three-digit SOC occupational categories. A conversion table developed by the U.S. Census (1986) was used to convert the 1980 categories into the 1970 ones. The 20 percent sample of the 1980 Census is particularly well suited for constructing this variable because it is such a large data set (about 20 million workers), averaging more than 40,000 individuals in each occupation. Thus it is the only data set large enough to produce reliable estimates of the proportion of women in each occupation. (The CPS, the only other data set that comes close, cannot produce reliable estimates for all occupational categories.)

Job attributes, derived from the fourth edition of the *Dictionary of Occupational Titles* by Ann R. Miller et al. (1980), were also included as independent variables in this analysis. Miller et al. reported on five variables, which describe the following characteristics of an occupation: the general educational requirement, the specific vocational preparation requirement, the strength requirement, the physical demands, and the undesirable environmental conditions associated with a job.

The other independent variables in the analysis were taken from the PSID. They include years of schooling completed; actual years of work experience and its square; years of tenure with current employer and its square; weeks sick last year; whether an individual worked part time last year; regional dummy variables; standard metropolitan statistical area (SMSA) dummy variables; race dummies for black, Hispanic, and other; dummies for marital status; the number of individuals under eighteen living at home; a dummy for the presence of such individuals; a dummy for the presence of individuals under five years of age; a dummy for the presence of a union contract in the firm where the individual works; dummies for being employed by the local, state, or federal government; and dummies for thirty-six two-digit Standard Industrial Classification (SIC) industry categories.

Empirical Results

This section first tests the hypothesis that, all else being equal, occupational segregation reduces earnings for workers in female-dominated jobs. It then presents estimates of the extent to which occupational segregation explains the male-female earnings gap. These findings are contrasted with those of Johnson and Solon, the only other researchers who used the analytic design employed here.

To test the aforementioned hypothesis, I estimated separate earnings equations for women and men which included a measure of the sex composition of an occupation as well as other control variables.[4] The results from these regressions are reported in table 4.2. I find that individual earnings are significantly depressed by the sex composition of an occupation, confirming my hypothesis. The estimated coefficient for the proportion of women in an occupation is –0.230 in the earnings regression for females (estimated standard error: 0.033) and –0.239 (estimated standard error: 0.040) in the earnings regression for males. Thus both women and men can expect to earn about 23 percent less in jobs held exclusively by women than in jobs held exclusively by men, even after controlling for productivity-related and industrial differences.

The estimated coefficients for the other variables in the analysis are similar to those found in other research. I found, for example, that the size of the estimated coefficients for education and job tenure are about the same for women and men but that the coefficient for work experience for men is about twice the magnitude of the coefficient for women. In addition, men with a bachelor of arts degree earn substantially more than women with the same degree.

Four dummy variables are used to describe an individual's marital status: married, widowed, separated, and divorced. Being single is the omitted variable. None of the dummy variables for a woman's marital status is statistically significant. For men, all of the dummy variables are positive, but only divorced men earn significantly more than single men. Three variables are used to control for differences in the number of children and the age of children in the home. Only one is significant: the presence of children under five years of age, which has a significantly positive effect on the earnings of males and a significantly negative effect on the earnings of females.

---

4. A disproportionate number of blacks are included in the PSID survey. To correct for this oversampling, I estimated weighted earnings equations, using the weights supplied by the PSID survey.

Table 4.2.   Means, Estimated Coefficients, and Standard Errors from Female and Male Log Wage Equations

	Female			Male		
Variables	*Means*	*Est. Coeff.*	*Standard Errors*	*Means*	*Est. Coeff.*	*Standard Errors*
Proportion female	0.6581	−0.2298[a]	0.0325	0.2356	−0.2385[a]	0.0398
Education	12.8161	0.3075[a]	0.0054	12.9146	0.0416[a]	0.0041
Work experience	12.1201	0.0132[a]	0.0025	19.4800	0.0306[a]	0.0025
Experience square	224.9897	−0.0003[a]	0.0001	526.9355	−0.0005[a]	0.0001
Tenure	6.3446	0.0224[a]	0.0028	9.8233	0.0180[a]	0.0024
Tenure square	82.2235	−0.0005[a]	0.0001	189.1731	−0.0003[a]	0.0001
B.A. degree	0.2072	0.0341	0.0266	0.2499	0.0853[a]	0.0233
Advanced degree	0.0500	0.0487	0.0336	0.0709	0.0480	0.0293
Weeks sick	1.0891	0.0003	0.0024	1.1166	−0.0013	0.0019
Part time last year	0.4896	−0.0771[a]	0.0145	0.2025	−0.0755[a]	0.0173
GED[b]	3.7828	0.1318[a]	0.0198	3.8726	0.0929[a]	0.0196
SVP[c]	5.1392	0.0187	0.0102	5.8387	0.0058	0.0092
Strength	1.9715	0.0045	0.0135	2.3505	−0.0318	0.0188
Physical demands	1.4957	0.0243[a]	0.0124	1.8120	−0.0456[a]	0.0110
Environment	0.2315	−0.0289	0.0170	0.6549	0.0234	0.0137
Northeast	0.2424	0.0028	0.0189	0.2278	0.0554[a]	0.0190
North central	0.2574	−0.0583[a]	0.0182	0.2941	0.0384[a]	0.0178
West	0.1881	0.0296	0.0205	0.1844	0.0827[a]	0.0207
Large SMSA	0.1749	0.1652[a]	0.0255	0.1641	0.1857[a]	0.0243
Medium SMSA	0.2794	0.1310[a]	0.0225	0.2719	0.1234[a]	0.0216
Small SMSA	0.1321	0.0691[a]	0.0259	0.1195	0.0579[a]	0.0255
Large non-SMSA	0.1258	0.0801[a]	0.0259	0.1344	0.0966[a]	0.0245
Medium non-SMSA	0.1558	0.0568[a]	0.0243	0.1642	0.0326	0.0233
Black	0.1264	−0.1167[a]	0.0213	0.0791	−0.1292[a]	0.0250
Hispanic	0.0236	−0.0076	0.0432	0.0302	−0.0724	0.0388
Other minority	0.0074	0.0350	0.0761	0.0103	0.0300	0.0653
Married	0.6063	0.0033	0.0204	0.7735	0.0360	0.0245
Widowed	0.0422	−0.0545	0.0380	0.0058	0.1469	0.0871
Separated	0.0420	0.0356	0.0363	0.0131	0.0852	0.0594
Divorced	0.1471	0.0107	0.0247	0.0747	0.0640[a]	0.0306

Table 4.2 (continued)

Variables	Female			Male		
	Means	*Est. Coeff.*	*Standard Errors*	*Means*	*Est. Coeff.*	*Standard Errors*
No. of children	0.8504	0.0103	0.0107	0.9277	−0.0008	0.0102
Children	0.4712	−0.0020	0.0244	0.4921	0.0009	0.0246
Children under 5	0.1739	−0.0451[a]	0.0199	0.2139	0.0495[a]	0.0200
Federal government	0.0349	0.2985[a]	0.0484	0.0375	0.1041	0.0707
State government	0.0863	0.0783	0.0404	0.0551	−0.0573	0.0682
Local government	0.1452	0.0555	0.0388	0.0978	−0.0795	0.0660
Union contract	0.1836	0.1454[a]	0.0189	0.2880	0.1894[a]	0.0168
Forest	0.0016	−0.0266	0.1578	0.0073	0.0135	0.0967
Mining	0.0013	0.2187	0.1774	0.0114	0.3147[a]	0.0864
Construction	0.0126	0.3007[a]	0.0660	0.0736	0.3102[a]	0.0670
Lumber	0.0076	0.2019[a]	0.0799	0.0204	0.1434	0.0767
Stone	0.0013	−0.1059	0.1797	0.0108	0.1063	0.0872
Metal	0.0099	0.2834[a]	0.0723	0.0408	0.1076	0.0700
Machinery	0.0206	0.2668[a]	0.0557	0.0541	0.2701[a]	0.0679
Electrical	0.0310	0.2148[a]	0.0498	0.0289	0.1836[a]	0.0725
Trans. equipment	0.0103	0.4033[a]	0.0716	0.0537	0.2754[a]	0.0687
Photo	0.0052	0.1569	0.0937	0.0097	0.1240	0.0889
Ordnance	0.0012	0.4391[a]	0.1835	0.0053	0.1760	0.1073
Misc. manufac- turing	0.0043	0.0300	0.1024	0.0059	0.0645	0.1029
Food	0.0063	0.4001[a]	0.0863	0.0241	0.0946	0.0748
Tobacco	0.0018	0.5070[a]	0.1524	0.0028	0.5624[a]	0.1343
Textile	0.0065	0.2169[a]	0.0853	0.0058	0.0490	0.1037
Apparel	0.0177	0.0349	0.0580	0.0032	−0.0453	0.1264
Paper	0.0042	0.1451	0.1038	0.0092	0.1902[a]	0.0903
Print	0.0155	0.0425	0.0609	0.0215	0.2260[a]	0.0755
Chemicals	0.0077	0.5147[a]	0.0791	0.0278	0.2324[a]	0.0730
Rubber	0.0024	0.1565	0.1333	0.0086	0.1154	0.0920
Leather	0.0058	−0.1722	0.0895	0.0023	−0.0163	0.1455
manufac- turing (n.e.c.)	0.0052	0.1310	0.0934	0.0078	0.1908[a]	0.0959
Transportation	0.0096	0.2823[a]	0.0723	0.0516	0.2499[a]	0.0683
Communica- tions	0.0162	0.3493[a]	0.0613	0.0256	0.2872[a]	0.0742
Utilities	0.0067	0.2511[a]	0.0851	0.0283	0.2856[a]	0.0731

Table 4.2 (continued)

Variables	Female			Male		
	Means	Est. Coeff.	Standard Errors	Means	Est. Coeff.	Standard Errors
Wholesale trade	0.0217	0.1141[a]	0.0546	0.0306	0.0730	0.0719
Retail trade	0.1404	−0.0990[a]	0.0371	0.0915	−0.0540	0.0652
Finance	0.0826	0.0677	0.0405	0.0344	0.1755[a]	0.0706
Business services	0.0277	0.0739	0.0507	0.0355	0.0011	0.0704
Entertainment	0.0009	0.1521	0.2084	0.0053	0.3611[a]	0.1066
Hospitals	0.0731	0.2436[a]	0.0424	0.0169	0.1731[a]	0.0795
Health services	0.0600	0.1015[a]	0.0428	0.0073	0.0641	0.0969
Educational services	0.0328	0.0372	0.0488	0.0115	−0.2333[a]	0.0865
Social services	0.0200	−0.0766	0.0561	0.0081	−0.3831[a]	0.0942
Professional services	0.0188	0.0317	0.0578	0.0156	0.2512[a]	0.0803
Misc. professional services	0.0038	0.3916[a]	0.1117	0.0023	0.2754	0.1453
Intercept	1.0000	0.5636[a]	0.0931	1.0000	0.8074[a]	0.1119
Adjusted R^2		.555			.584	
n		2411			2616	

[a]$P < .05$
[b]General educational development.
[c]Specific vocational preparation.

Thirty-six two-digit SIC industry dummy variables are included in the analysis; the personal services industry is the omitted variable. Most men and women earn more if they are employed in industries other than personal services. Men, however, earn significantly less in social and educational services, whereas women earn significantly less in retail trade.

The male-female earnings gap can be divided into five components. The first component measures the effect of differences in the sex composition of an occupation on this gap. The second accounts for differences between women and men in education and experience. The third measures the effect of differences between women and men in the industries in which they work. The fourth measures the impact of sex-based differences in all other factors. The final component measures the amount unexplained by differences in these characteristics. This division is particularly useful in that it separates the effect of occupational segregation from the other effects most

Table 4.3.   Percentage of Male-Female Pay Gap Accounted for by
Differences in Characteristics[a]

Controls	PSID			Johnson and Solon		
	Coefficients (F)	Coefficients (M)	Average	(F)	(M)	Average
Proportion of women in occupation	22.9	23.8	23.3	11.4	21.2	16.3
Education and experience	10.3	23.7	17.0	2.1	3.2	2.7
Industry	19.9	17.1	18.5	15.3	15.1	15.2
Others[b]	13.1	9.9	11.5	12.0	15.5	13.8
Unexplained	33.8	25.5	29.7	59.2	45.0	52.1

[a]Percentage of pay gap explained by characteristics using male coefficients is derived
by:

$$b_{mj} (Z_{mj} - Z_{fj}) \ / \ (ln \ w_m - ln \ w_f)$$

expressed as a percent, where Z_{mj} and Z_{fj} are the sample mean for men and women on
a given variable j. b_{mj} are the male regression coefficients. The figure using female
coefficients is the same except that b_{mj} is replaced by b_{fj}, the female regression coefficients. The average is equal to the two figures added together and divided by two.

[b]Includes measures of job attributes, marital status, children, regional and urban status, race and ethnicity, union status, government employment, part-time work, and
weeks sick last year.

frequently cited as contributing significantly to the earnings gap. Table 4.3 reports the proportion of the sex-based earnings gap that is
explained by each of these components.

Table 4.3 shows that the sex composition of an occupation accounts
for an average 23 percent of the male-female earnings gap. Industrial segregation explains 19 percent. Once these factors are controlled for, differences in education and experience account for 17
percent of the earnings gap and differences in the other factors explain 12 percent. Thirty percent of the earnings gap is unexplained
by these variables.

In contrast, Johnson and Solon claimed that the sex composition of
an occupation played a much smaller role in explaining male-female
pay differences. They argued that a more important factor was the
difference in the industrial distribution of women and men. Using
Johnson and Solon's data, I ascertained the relative contribution of
these factors in maintaining the earnings disparity between women
and men. These findings are reported in table 4.3. As shown, differences in the sex composition of an occupation account for 16 percent
of the sex-based earnings gap, while industrial differences account

for 15 percent. Consequently, Johnson and Solon's empirical analysis shows occupational segregation and industrial segregation are equally important in reducing the relative earnings of women. In contrast, my research, using PSID data, shows that occupational segregation is more important than industrial segregation in accounting for this disparity. Thus it is difficult to conclude from these analyses that occupational segregation plays a less significant role than industrial segregation in the determination of relative wages.

Table 4.3 also shows that differences in variables measuring education and experience explain only 3 percent of the pay gap in Johnson and Solon's analysis. In contrast, in my analysis these variables explain 17 percent of the gap. This difference arises because Johnson and Solon used less precise measures of education and work experience. For example, they did not have measures for actual work experience or tenure. Instead, they used potential work experience (i.e., age-education-sex). When I used the same measures of education and work experience (i.e., education, potential work experience, and its square), my results were the same as theirs. Similarly, Johnson and Solon used only twenty industry dummy variables in their analysis whereas I employed thirty-six such variables. Thus it is not surprising that I explain more of the earnings gap by differences in industry variables than Johnson and Solon do. Replacing these thirty-six variables with twenty that are quite similar to those used by Johnson and Solon, I found that 15.6 percent of the earnings gap was explained by this smaller set of industry variables, a figure quite similar to that found by Johnson and Solon (15.2 percent).

The independent factors other than education, work experience, industrial distribution, and occupation segregation employed by Johnson and Solon explain more of the sex-based earnings gap than the remaining measures in my analysis. This discrepancy occurs in part because Johnson and Solon included more explanatory variables that do not specifically measure education, experience, industrial distribution, or occupational segregation. They included three measures of part-time status, for example, whereas I included only one. They included two dummy variables for whether an individual was currently working part time voluntarily or involuntarily. They also included a variable for the proportion of part-time workers in an individual's occupation. Moreover, the PSID survey does not ask respondents how many hours they are currently working, only how many they worked last year. The variable in my analysis measuring part-time work is based on this question and thus is measured less precisely than the variables Johnson and Solon used.

In addition, as shown in table 4.3, Johnson and Solon's analysis leaves 52 percent of the sex-based earnings gap unexplained. In contrast, my analysis leaves only 30 percent unexplained. Consequently, the set of control variables employed in my analysis explains more of the discrepancy in earnings than that employed by Johnson and Solon.

Finally, as pointed out earlier, there is a large discrepancy between my results and those of Johnson and Solon regarding the relative contribution of the sex composition of an occupation to the sex-based earnings gap. This variable explains 23 percent of the male-female earnings gap in my analysis but only 16 percent of the gap in Johnson and Solon's analysis. Although Johnson and Solon measure this variable using annual CPS data and I use Census data, this difference does not explain the disparity in our findings. This was determined by reestimating the earnings equations described above and replacing the Census-based measure of occupational segregation with the measure employed by Johnson and Solon (which Johnson and Solon generously provided). Using these estimated earnings regressions, I found that their measure of the sex composition of an occupation explained 21 percent of the sex-based earnings gap. This figure is slightly smaller than my finding (23 percent) but substantially larger than theirs (16 percent).

Two other explanations can be given for the differences in the findings. First, one would expect different results because different control variables were used in each study. Adding control variables that negatively (or positively) affect earnings and are positively (or negatively) correlated with the proportion of women in an occupation will reduce the estimated coefficient for this latter variable. For example, Johnson and Solon included a variable that measures the proportion of part-time workers in an occupation, and I do not. This variable fits the aforementioned description, and thus a smaller effect of occupational segregation on relative earnings is expected. A second reason for these disparate findings is that data from different years were examined: one study examined data for 1978; the other examined data for 1984. During this period, employment distributions changed, which possibly contributes to the differences in the estimated coefficients.

I also examined simple earnings regressions for women and men, which include the proportion of women in an occupation as the only independent variable. These estimates describe the gross relationship between individual earnings and the sex composition of an occupation. Based on this analysis, I found yet another difference between my results and those reported by Johnson and Solon. They also estimated simple earnings regressions for women and men and found that both estimated coefficients for the proportion of women in an occupation were quite large (−.343 for men and −.244 for women). After other independent variables were included in their analysis, they found that these estimates declined by more than one-half. In my analysis, the estimated coefficients from the simple earnings regressions are quite different for women and men. The estimated coefficient for the sex composition of an occupation is −0.160 for men (estimated standard error: 0.045) and −0.329 (0.034) for women. Thus, according to this simple earnings equation, men earn 16 percent less in a female-dominated occupation than in a male-dominated occupation. Women earn 33 percent less. After other independent variables are included in the analysis, the estimated coefficient for this variable increases to −0.239 for men and decreases to −0.230 for women (these figures are reported in table 4.1). Thus the coefficient for males increases by about 50 percent and the coefficient for females decreases by about 30 percent.

To understand why the estimated coefficient for the proportion of women increases in the earnings equation for men and decreases in the earnings equation for women, I decomposed the difference between the simple and full regression estimates. These results are reported in table 4.4. I found, as Johnson and Solon did, that adding industry dummy variables decreased the estimated coefficient for men. This is not surprising in that most of the industry dummy variables increase earnings and are negatively correlated with the percentage of workers in an occupation who are female. Thus, leaving them out of the analysis causes the estimated coefficient for the sex composition of an occupation to overestimate the relationship between earnings and occupational segregation. I also found, however, that education and experience increased the estimated coefficient by an equivalent amount, a much larger effect for these variables than Johnson and Solon found. Although I found a negative correlation between actual work experience (and tenure) and the percentage of workers in an occupation who are female, the variables measuring education, completion of a bachelor of arts degree, and completion of an advanced degree were positively correlated with this variable. Because these variables increase earnings, leaving them out of the analysis causes the estimated coefficient for the sex composition of an occupation to underestimate the relationship between this variable and earnings. The other independent variables in the analysis increase (or decrease) the estimated coefficient for the sex composition of an occupation in much the same way as Johnson and Solon found. Consequently, the differences in the measures of education and work

Table 4.4   Decomposition of the Influence of Control Variables on the
Estimation of the Coefficient for the Proportion Female in an Occupation

| | PSID | | Johnson and Solon | |
Controls	F	M	F	M
Total effect[a]	−.099	.079	−.153	−.173
Industry	−.023	−.150	−.083	−.152
Education and experience	−.020	.131	−.024	.024
Job characteristics	−.013	.146	−.012	.034
Part-time status	−.019	−.010	−.009	−.019
Union status	−.015	−.021	−.022	−.029
Marital status and kids	−.002	−.006	−.003	−.034
Region and SMSA variables	−.003	.013	.002	.017
Race	−.0003	−.007	−.001	−.003
Government employment	−.002	−.018	−.001	−.015

[a]The estimated coefficient for proportion female from the simple regression minus the estimated coefficient for proportion female from the full model.

experience explain most of the differences between my results from the decomposition of the earnings equations for males and those reported by Johnson and Solon.

I found that the estimated coefficient for women declined by three-tenths; Johnson and Solon's figure is one-half. The industry dummy variables contribute to this reduction, but other variables also play a role, including education, work experience, and union status. These results are not surprising, for these variables are negatively correlated with the percentage of workers in an occupation who are female and significantly affect women's earnings. Thus, in the simple equation, the estimated coefficient for the percentage of workers who are female will overestimate the relationship between this variable and earnings.

Conclusions

A review of both the theoretical and empirical literature on the relationship between occupational segregation and earnings reveals that neither body of literature is satisfactory. The theoretical literature is incomplete, and the empirical literature is often plagued with biases. Nonetheless, these studies indicate that 10 to 30 percent of the male-female earnings gap is due to the sex composition of an occupation. My own research demonstrates that employment in a job held predominantly by women reduces individual earnings significantly. Furthermore, this particular variable explains 23 percent of the male-female earnings disparity. Thus the impact of this variable on earnings is not only significant but substantial. These results suggest that comparable worth legislation could remedy an important component of the sex-based earnings gap.

DISCUSSION

JUDITH M. GERSON

Although this paper is replete with important findings, their lack of consistency forces the author to draw only the most tentative of conclusions. The sociological reader will find, however, that the absence of definitive results provides an opportunity to suggest paths for future research.

Elaine Sorensen begins her analysis with a discussion of two theoretical discrimination theories that purportedly explain occupational sex composition. The first of these theories, the crowding model, argues that "because of discrimination, women and men are segregated into different occupations and that those doing women's work earn less than those doing men's work even though they are equally productive." The crowding model seems to be essentially a structural model that uses an implicit double standard to explain the lower wages in female-dominated jobs. Occupational sex segregation occurs in male-dominated jobs as well. Yet only in female-dominated occupations are wages depressed. Furthermore, although women's jobs are more crowded than men's, this fact does not account for the growth and shrinkage of various job categories and industrial sectors. In particular, the expansion of traditionally female-dominated jobs in the service sector suggests that the demand for labor is increasing. The crowding of women into sales jobs, for example, is not necessarily isomorphic with the crowding of men in steel manufacturing jobs (England and Farkas 1986). Finally, the crowding model should be extended and used to analyze longitudinal data. Trend studies would facilitate an understanding of the historic causality of the interrelationship between declines in wages and increases in the proportion of women in a job category. Do wages drop in anticipation of more women entering an occupation, or do falling wages drive men out and/or pull women in? What is the tipping point of "too many women" in a given occupational category within a particular industrial sector at a given point in time? Does that tipping point vary by occupation, industry, or historical period? In other words, the crowding model needs to be explored further with longitudinal data to specify the causal ordering of female-dominated jobs and decreasing wages.

The second major theory, the institutional model, argues that the "pricing and allocation of labor is governed by a set of rules and customs rather than by direct supply-and-demand considerations." But rather than explain the processes by which wage rates are set, it describes them. Researchers adopting this perspective have been unable heretofore to specify how these norms and values actually function to depress wages in female-dominated occupations. Attempts to explain social processes become tautological as researchers resort to understanding the causal roots of the problem in norms or customs. It may be possible to begin to resolve the circularity of reasoning in this approach by recognizing explicitly that actual people are involved. People make decisions to apply for some jobs rather than others, and actual people—not dominant values—make decisions concerning wage rates. People act with the knowledge of cultural norms and customs. Norms and values shape the behaviors and attitudes of people; they do not determine them. More in-depth studies of the processes of occupational "choice" and hiring decisions will perhaps facilitate a more precise explanation of the causal ordering of these social processes.

The empirical data generally indicate that occupational sex segregation actually affects the earnings of all workers. For the sociologist studying gender, these findings are of great interest for several reasons. The first, emphasized by Sorensen, is that there are large differences among some previous studies as well as between her own work and earlier work by others (e.g., Johnson and Solon 1984). Sorensen correctly attributes the reasons for these differences to methodological dissimilarities among these research endeavors. Authors used different data sets, different time periods, different operationalizations of independent and dependent variables, and so on. Reviewing these studies, I remain relatively unperturbed by the lack of reliability among estimations. These studies by and large point to the existence of an effect of the sex composition of occupations on pay levels even after other relevant job, industrial, and demographic characteristics have been entered into the equations. I do not necessarily expect to see coefficients of equal or near-equal magnitude. Occupational sex segregation may be a persistent phenomenon in this society, but it is not a constant. A comprehensive analysis of sex differences in earnings must therefore incorporate an understanding of industrial segmentation and job segregation by sex as well as by occupational sex segregation (Parcel and Mueller 1983). These factors in addition to individual-level human capital characteristics need to be specified to evaluate the direct and indirect effects of occupational sex segregation on wage rates.

The second point emanating from the empirical literature that I want to emphasize is the differential consequences of occupational sex segregation for women and men. Though these differences are not identical across all studies, there is some indication that men's wages in female-dominated jobs are depressed more than women's. In other words, there may be a gender effect in occupational sex segregation. Being a male or female may have a differential impact on wage rates even within an occupational category. While the empirical evidence is preliminary at this moment, we need to investigate this effect in greater detail.

Finally, investigators studying the effects of occupational sex composition on wages would be well served to consider the interaction effects of sex with age, race, and marital status as well as other status and occupational characteristics. Previous research has demonstrated, for example, a greater decline in occupational sex segregation among younger workers than among older workers and in professional occupations than in occupations generally (Beller 1984; Jacobs 1985). Moreover, other researchers have found a race and sex effect in predictions of the wages of black women (Parcel and Mueller 1983). Thus we need to ascertain what effect, if any, these variables have on wage rates both independently and in interaction with sex. This knowledge will facilitate a realistic understanding of the potential for equalizing wages by implementing comparable worth policies as well as the limitations of such strategies for certain groups of workers.

Sorensen concludes her paper by stating that her research has shown that the sex composition of an occupation has a significant effect on earnings, thereby validating comparable worth remedies. I would like to underscore this conclusion. The problem of unequal pay is a challenging one for social scientists. Its causes are multifaceted and complex. Yet the intractability of the problem should neither dissuade researchers from continuing attempts to specify an explanatory model nor discourage the courts from implementing comparable worth remedies when appropriate.

CLAUDIA GOLDIN

The central finding of Elaine Sorensen's paper is that "both women and men can expect to earn . . . 23 percent less in jobs held exclusively by women than in jobs held exclusively by men, even after controlling for productivity-related and industrial differences [between women and men]." Sorensen's data integrate those in several data sets: the 1984 Panel Study of Income Dynamics yields the rich work experience, education, and family characteristics variables for the individual observations; the 1980 Census provides the key percentage female variable for each occupation (that is, the percentage of workers who are female); and the 1980 *Dictionary of Occupational Titles* gives various occupational characteristics. Should Sorensen's central finding surprise us, and what should be done about it?

First, should we be surprised? Various earnings function or "wage discrimination" studies have demonstrated that one cannot explain more than 40 to 50 percent, if even that, of the logarithmic wage gap between male and female workers using conventional variables such as education, experience, marital status, and others included in Sorensen's study. Further, as the definition of an occupation narrows, such as at the three-digit level used here, differences in pay by sex within occupations become very small. Most pay differences within narrowly defined occupations are accounted for by differences in attributes. So it must be the case that differences in wages by sex that are unexplained by conventional variables are more prominent across occupations than they are within occupations and therefore that they are correlated with the variable percentage female.

And what of the magnitude of the coefficient? It is somewhat larger than that in the article by George Johnson and Gary Solon (1986) that Sorensen uses as a bench mark for comparison, but it is in the ball park. They find an average explanatory power of 16 percent, 21 percent in the equation for females and 11 percent in the equation for males.[1] Several differences exist between the two studies that might explain the somewhat diverse results, but Sorensen's careful examination of the possibilities leads one to conclude otherwise. The most convincing evidence that the data sets and not the definitions of the variables or the variables themselves must be the ultimate culprits is the following. Even in an equation containing only the vari-

---

1. The authors rely on somewhat different coefficients in their final computations and report that, on average, 13.5 percent is explained by the percentage female variable, 19 percent in the equation for females and 8 percent in the equation for males.

able percentage female regressed on the wages of females and males, Johnson and Solon's data produce −24.4 percent for the females and −34.3 percent for the males, while Sorensen's data yield −33 percent for the females and −16 percent for the males.

Sorensen's results are, however, considerably larger than those in a study by Randall Filer (1987).[2] Filer eliminates entirely the impact of the percentage female in the equations for both males and females by accounting for a wide variety of job characteristics, such as responsibility, effort, working conditions, and fringe benefits. Yet, in the absence of these additional variables, the coefficients for the percentage female are similar to those in Sorensen's study, which also includes several occupational characteristics, such as strength required, physical demands, and environment. Whether or not one wants to account for the many additional characteristics in Filer's study, which negate the impact of the percentage female, will depend on what the characteristics measure. Consider the following examples.

In the late nineteenth century when most typists were men, typing was considered both physically and mentally too strenuous for women workers. Yet, in the absence of technological change, typing rapidly became the quintessential female occupation, and its required skills suddenly became manual dexterity, not the capacity for arduous labor (Davies 1982). Also during the late nineteenth century, inherently dirty industries, such as meatpacking, were considered inappropriate for women workers, and only after the industries became cleaner or only when their dirty aspects could be isolated in separate rooms were women hired. Thus, although Filer's study appears to negate Sorensen's results, it may add many characteristics that are inappropriate. The characteristics may be subjective and thus determined by the dominant sex of the occupation, as in the typing example, or the characteristics may lead to the exclusion of women, as in the meatpacking case. Nonetheless, the additional characteristics in Filer's study and his research deserve further thought and attention.

In sum, I am not surprised at Sorensen's finding in principle or with its magnitude. That said, let me correct several possible misinterpretations. While the coefficient on proportion female is −0.23, it is somewhat misleading to state that it implies a 23 percent drop in earnings. That result holds only as one moves from no women in an

---

2. Filer uses 430 occupations rather than the individual-level data Sorensen employs but matches them to individual-level characteristics that are similar to those in Sorensen's study.

occupation to all women—a jump from 0 to 1. Rather than referring to large changes that span the entire possible range, the coefficient can be more appropriately expressed in other more conventional manners.

First, as an elasticity, the coefficient becomes −0.12 or about minus one-eighth, evaluated around a mean of 0.5, for the proportion female. That is, the wages of females would drop by 1.2 percent for every 10 percent increase in the percentage female. Second, it can be expressed as the net change in the wage rate for each 10 percentage point increase in the percentage female. Using this expression, it becomes 15 cents per hour, or 2.3 percent.[3] That is, when the percentage female increases by 10 percentage points, the wage drops by 15 cents per hour. Expressed in these more standard manners, as a response to a small change, the coefficient −0.23 takes on a clearer and more informative meaning.

Another possible misconception is that a comparable worth policy can eliminate much of the difference, however measured, between the earnings of equally trained males and females across the sex-stratified occupational distribution. Comparable worth legislation in the United States would affect only within-firm or within-state government employees. Because much of the difference isolated by Sorensen's study is likely caused by across-firm differences, a comparable worth policy might not serve to eliminate much of the gap.

While the remainder of my remarks focus on the implications of the coefficient on the percentage female, one other result in table 4.2 should be highlighted: the 12 to 13 percent decrease in hourly earnings for black men and women, given all other factors. These results imply further aspects of discrimination and the need for effective antidiscrimination legislation.

Given that one ought not be surprised by the central finding in principle or with its magnitude, what should be done about it? Because the appropriate remedy will depend on what is causing the coefficient on the percentage female to be negative, I turn now to a discussion of one possible explanation.

Some additional results in a paper by June O'Neill (1983) will be helpful in this regard.[4] That paper uses a very similar methodology;

---

3. The calculation uses the $6.62 per hour wage for females given by Sorensen, (*ln* 6.62 = 1.89) and is computed around an initial starting point of 50 percent female.

4. O'Neill uses both the 1978 National Longitudinal Survey and the 1980 Current Population Survey in various portions of the paper. The results to which I refer concern only the 1978 NLS because it includes variables similar to those used by Sorensen.

the data set is the National Longitudinal Survey, while the one here is the Panel Study of Income Dynamics, and the year of the data is 1978, not 1984. But the results are not very different from those in Sorensen's paper.

O'Neill did use a slightly more elaborate functional form for the percentage female variable and found important nonlinearities in the relationship between the hourly wage of women and the proportion female. The relationship between the hourly wage and the proportion female is first negative, moving from 0 to 0.5, but it is then positive, moving from 0.5 to 1. The finding is particularly strong among young college-educated women. Thus many of the highest paid occupations are extremely sex-segregated, as are many of the lowest paid occupations. It suggests that if the crowding model is operating, it is a rather different one than that originally conceived by Barbara Bergmann and others (see, for example, Bergmann 1986); women, it seems, are crowded into both the lower and the upper tails of the wage distribution.

How can we make sense of these results and formulate the appropriate remedy? Not by further estimations, but instead by pulling out testable propositions from rather simple theories of discrimination in competitive markets. We may be able to make some progress by expanding on Gary Becker's original model of discrimination (1957) and making tastes for discrimination depend on how male workers perceive a woman in their occupation to affect their status. The model I have in mind is historical and begins long ago when various gender-based characteristics, as well as custom and tradition, affected productivity to a considerable extent, far more than they eventually did.

The main premise is quite simple.[5] Men will prefer that women not be hired in their occupation if the employment of women signals that the skills required for the occupation have been degraded, that is, if the employment of women reduces the status of men in that occupation. The key to the model is that certain occupations will lose status if a woman is hired, while others will not. Which do and which do not depends on the magnitude of the characteristic or attribute (skill, education, strength) initially required for the occupation. Those that lose status have attributes above the median value of the characteristic in the female population. The value of the required attribute for each occupation is initially public knowledge; in 1800, for example, everyone knew that shoemakers and weavers were skilled artisans. But the

---

5. The full model can be found in Goldin 1988.

skills demanded can, and did, change over time with technological change. Precisely how they change is private knowledge, but it is inferred from the composition of the work force. Thus, if the occupation initially requires a level of skill higher than that of the median woman, the hiring of a woman will reduce the status of men in the occupation, unless her particular skills are public knowledge.

More formally, assume two distributions of some single-valued human capital (C) attribute, one for males and one for females, and also assume that the median values are known to all. Wages are a simple function of C, and an occupation is defined as a level of C; thus there can be a male and a female occupation for each level of C. Initially, all men are employed, and women then begin to enter the labor force.

How will a woman be greeted in each occupation if she tries to enter with her particular level of C? The answer is that it will depend. If she tries to enter an occupation for which the current level of C is greater than the median for all females, men will find their status "polluted," shall I say, by the presence of a woman. Their status in the occupation will be depressed by the new information revealed by the presence of a woman, because women, on average, have lower C than do men. Even if the occupation does not change, in some fashion, all individuals outside the occupation will view the presence of women as a signal that the requisite skills have been degraded, because information about the skills of a particular entrant and those required by the occupation, after the initial period, is private knowledge. But if, instead, the current value of C is less than the median for women, men will not care; indeed, their status will be enhanced by the presence of women. Thus certain men will demand a premium to work in an occupation that also contains women, while some will not. As long as occupations can be created in a virtually costless fashion, employers will not have to pay the premium to integrate but will instead create sex-segregated occupations above the median value of the attribute for females.

The result is that occupations will be segregated by sex in a non-monotonic fashion with respect to the attribute C. One can reasonably begin with the two distributions—one for females and the other for males—overlapping but with that for females being somewhat shifted down from that for males. The lowest paid workers will be in all-female occupations, middling-income workers will be in integrated ones, above middling-paid workers will be segregated by sex, and, finally, the highest paid workers will be in all-male occupations. Thus, among female workers both the lowest and the highest paid will be in completely sex-segregated occupations while those somewhere in the middle will be in integrated occupations.

Economic progress shifts the female distribution of C closer to the male distribution (e.g., technological change reduces the need for strength, education substitutes brain power for muscle, and custom and tradition atrophy with economic progress). The response to these shifts highlights the importance of historical notions of women's work and men's work. Some jobs will be considered "men's," and there may be resistance to integration even though these jobs may eventually become integrated. Also, the market may respond slowly in creating jobs in the upper tail of the female distribution. Further, women may prepare for what were traditionally female jobs even though these jobs do not fully utilize new levels of formal schooling.

The model thus predicts that crowding, if it does occur, will be in the upper tail of the female distribution, not the lower tail. This so-called crowding may not have any wage effects, however, even though individuals will be improperly placed in jobs. Women will receive too low a return on human capital, and "wage discrimination" measures will reflect this. But the jobs receive the correct wage for the skill demanded, and a Hay point analysis, for example, will not reveal any labor market inefficiency. Comparable worth legislation will then be incapable of redressing the problem, but affirmative action would be an appropriate remedy. Note that many of the propositions that stem from this simple model are consistent with the estimation in Sorensen's paper and in that by O'Neill, particularly that the relationship between the percentage female and wages is nonmonotonic. That is, the model predicts that those occupations at the lowest and highest ends of the wage scale will have a high percentage of workers who are female, while occupations with both men and women will tend to be in the middle (the model predicts these jobs are just below the median for females). The coefficient on the percentage female will be negative in the equation for males, as in Sorensen's study, and is likely to be negative in the equation for females as well.[6] The propositions of the model are also consistent with the history of gender differences in the economy and with the manner in which gender distinctions are reinforced over time.[7]

---

6. Whether or not the coefficient on the percentage of females will be negative depends on the position of the underlying quadratic and the distribution of the labor force across occupations.

7. In Goldin 1988, several data sets indicate that clerical occupations around 1940 were sex-segregated in a manner consistent with many of the propositions of the model.

Let me end by calling for more thought about what is being estimated. Until there is, we will not be able to interpret the results of
empirical studies even as carefully executed as that by Elaine Sorensen in light of a serious proposal for comparable worth.

5

EMPIRICAL CONSEQUENCES OF COMPARABLE WORTH

Ronald G. Ehrenberg

A LTHOUGH some efforts to implement comparable worth have taken place in the private sector, the major push has occurred in state and local governments, a sector of the economy in which union membership is growing and a large proportion of the employees are women. Starting with a 1974 state of Washington study, several states have undertaken formal job evaluation studies to see how their compensation systems mesh with the principle of comparable worth, and several state and local governments have begun to implement comparable worth either through the legislative or collective bargaining process (see Ehrenberg and Smith 1987a, tables 10.1 and 10.2).

Although proponents and opponents of comparable worth continue to debate the legitimacy of the concept, to some extent events have passed them by. Protestations of economists to the contrary, the concept of comparable worth has become widely accepted in the public sector of some states, raising the policy question of whether the concept should be extended to other public employees in the state and local sectors and to the federal and private sectors. While debate on this issue will undoubtedly continue to be both emotionally charged and politically motivated, rational decision making must include an

I am grateful to the authors of papers that were still in preliminary form, including several that were presented at a September 1987 National Academy of Science Authors' Workshop Panel on Pay Equity, for permitting me to read and cite their works. Revised versions of the NAS papers will appear in Michael and Hartmann (forthcoming).

Without implicating them for what remains, I am grateful to Francine Blau, Pamela Cain, Janice Madden, John Pencavel, Robert Smith, Elaine Sorensen, and two anonymous referees for their comments on earlier versions of this paper.

evaluation of what the empirical consequences of comparable worth are likely to be. Decision makers in both the legislative and collective bargaining processes need to know, for example, whether implementation of comparable worth can be expected to improve the female-male earnings ratios significantly, whether it would lead to a decline in the employment of women, whether it would induce more women to enter the labor force, whether it would help or hinder the occupational mobility of women and reduce occupational segmentation, and who would "win" and who would "lose."

To help focus subsequent debate, this paper presents a nontechnical survey of the small but growing empirical literature by economists on the consequences of comparable worth. I discuss in turn studies of the consequences of comparable worth on the male-female earnings gap, of its potential to affect adversely the employment of women, of its effects on the labor supply and occupational mobility of women, and of its effects on women *and* their families as a group. The survey is critical in nature and points to areas in which research is needed.

There are several important empirical issues relevant to future policy debate that I do not discuss. These include the existence of sex bias in describing or evaluating jobs, the difficulty (some would argue impossibility) of devising a single evaluation scheme that can meaningfully compare the "worth" of all employees in a single firm, and the problem of rater reliability; these are all issues that have been, and will be, addressed by noneconomists. I also do not discuss a key theoretical issue of concern to economists, namely, whether it makes any sense to speak of the worth of a job independent of labor market conditions. Rather, my focus is solely on empirical studies of the consequences of implementing a comparable worth policy.

Effect on Earnings Gap

Estimates of whether implementing comparable worth would have a significant effect on the gap between the average earnings of females and the average earnings of males have been both ex ante and ex post in nature. Ex ante studies (Ehrenberg and Smith 1987a; Sorensen 1986, 1987a, 1987b; Johnson and Solon 1986; Aldrich and Buchele 1986; and Smith 1988) use cross-section data to estimate how much women's wages would increase if comparable worth were implemented in a way the authors specify. Ex post studies (Kahn 1987; Killingsworth 1987a, 1987b; and Orazem and Matilla 1987) try to infer what has happened to the earnings of males and females after the *actual* implementation of comparable worth–type pay adjustments in the public sector. I discuss each type of study in turn.

Ex Ante Studies.   Most, but not all, states have conducted job evaluations for their employees based on the factor point method (Treiman 1979). The characteristics of jobs are described, and raters then assign point scores to each job on a number of dimensions. In the widely used Hay point system, for example, developed by Hay Associates, these dimensions are know-how, problem solving, accountability, and working conditions. In another widely used system, developed by Norman D. Willis and Associates, the dimensions are knowledge and skill, mental demand, accountability, and working conditions. The points a job receives for each category are then summed to get a total score, or measure of worth for the job.

Assuming that the principle of comparable worth requires that jobs of equal worth be paid equal wages, one can compute a comparable worth wage gap (CWWG), or estimate of how much, on average, wage levels in female-dominated jobs (typically taken to be those that employ at least 70 percent females) would have to be increased to achieve equal wage levels with equally rated male-dominated jobs (taken to be those that employ at least 70 percent males): First, estimate a wage equation in which a measure of the occupational wage (e.g., the starting wage scale, the mid-range wage scale, or the maximum wage scale in the occupation) in male-dominated jobs is specified to be a function of only the occupation's total factor point score. Next, compute, in percentage terms, how much the actual wage in each female-dominated job lies below this estimated male wage equation; this is an estimate of the magnitude of the comparable worth wage adjustment required in each occupation. Finally, weight each of these individual occupational wage adjustments by the share of employees in each occupation and then aggregate across the female-dominated occupations to come up with the CWWG.

This was the approach followed by Ronald G. Ehrenberg and Robert S. Smith (1987a) and Elaine Sorensen (1987a), who together studied pay systems for state government employees in five states and local government employees in one municipality *prior* to any implementation of comparable worth in the jurisdictions. Of course, in implementing the methodology described above, the researchers had to decide which wage measures to use (Sorensen used a single measure; Ehrenberg and Smith experimented with starting, mid-range, and maximum salaries), which functional form to use to describe the wages of males (Sorensen used a linear equation, Ehrenberg and

Table 5.1. Estimates of Comparable Worth Wage Gaps (CWWG) for State Employees in Selected States and Municipal Employees in San Jose[a]

Study	Jurisdiction	Evaluation System	Estimated CWWG
Ehrenberg & Smith (1986)	Minnesota (1981)	Hay	14.6–20.0%
	Washington (1974)	Willis	21.9–23.9
	Connecticut (1980)	Willis	15.4–20.2
Sorensen (1987a)	Iowa (1983)	Arthur Young	15.9
	Michigan (early 1980s)	Arthur Young	17.5
	Minnesota (1981)	Hay	21.4
	San Jose (1982)	Hay	25.5
	Washington (1983)	Willis	33.5

[a]The larger estimate observed by Sorensen for the state of Washington than those obtained by Ehrenberg and Smith may reflect the latter's use of data from different years (1983 versus 1974).

Smith experimented with linear and loglinear functional forms), and whether to enter the four individual factor point scores rather than the total score as predictors in the male wage equation (Ehrenberg and Smith experimented with the four-factor point scores because this allowed the existing male-dominated occupational structure to determine the marginal value the state placed on an additional point in each of the four categories, rather than assuming that only total factor points affected wages).

The results of the two studies are summarized in table 5.1. CWWGs in the range of 15.4 to 33.5 percent were found for the six jurisdictions. The range of estimates for each state in the Ehrenberg and Smith study occurred because of all the experimentation they did. In each case, however, their estimates were fairly robust to the methods used.

Given these estimates, one can compute the effect of making such comparable worth wage adjustments on the relative earnings of men and women by computing hypothetical wages for all female and male employees after such adjustments (assuming these adjustments are made only in female-dominated occupations and are given to employees of *both* sexes employed in these occupations) and then contrasting the ratio of average female to average male wages after the adjustments to the ones that existed before. This was the procedure followed by Sorensen: the unweighted average (across the six jurisdictions) earnings ratio observed before the hypothetical adjustments was 76 percent, whereas it was 87 percent after the adjustment. Sorensen thus concluded that, on average, such comparable worth wage adjustments would reduce the female-male earnings gap for *government employees* in these jurisdictions by about 45 percent (11/24).

For several reasons, one must be cautious in drawing conclusions from these numbers about the likely effects of implementing comparable worth for state employees. First, in some of the states (e.g., Washington), the job evaluations covered only a sample of state employee occupations; the results may not generalize to other state employee groups. Second, such wage adjustments raise total labor costs (on average Sorensen computes this increase to be 8 percent of payroll), which, along with the changing relative costs across occupations, may cause the level and composition of employment across both male-dominated and female-dominated occupations to change. Sorensen implicitly assumes no such changes would occur. Finally, given the political nature of both the collective bargaining and legislative processes and the constant pressure by groups to improve their job evaluation scores (see Ehrenberg and Smith 1987a, n. 17), there is reason to believe that actual comparable worth wage adjustments would not approach the magnitudes described above. Indeed, as we shall see below, several studies suggest that in practice such adjustments have been much smaller in several states.

Private-sector ex ante studies, such as those by George Johnson and Gary Solon (1986), Sorensen (1987b), Mark Aldrich and Robert Buchele (1986), and Robert S. Smith (1988), have adopted somewhat different approaches. Johnson and Solon use a large national sample of both private- and public-sector workers taken from the May 1978 Current Population Survey and estimate wage equations for males and females as functions of the individuals' personal characteristics (e.g., age), industry dummy variables, occupational characteristics variables (developed by the National Research Council), and a variable that measures the percentage of the workers in an occupation who are female. In such wage equations, a larger share of female employees in an occupation is associated with lower wages.

Johnson and Solon then *interpret* the concept of comparable worth to mean that it would be illegal to have this share influence wages and simulate how much the average female-male wage gap would be reduced if the coefficients of the female share were set at zero. Depending on the specification they use, an overall female-male wage differential of roughly 41 percent is estimated to decline by 3 to 8 percent when this restriction is imposed. Johnson and Solon thus estimate that comparable worth would reduce the overall wage gap by at most one-tenth to one-fifth.

Aldrich and Buchele, who used a different sample of data, the National Longitudinal Surveys, undertook a similar calculation and found that comparable worth would "reduce the male-female wage gap by 15 to 20 percent" (Aldrich and Buchele 1986, 148). So their estimate and that of Johnson and Solon are fairly consistent.

Finally, Sorensen (1987b) extends and replicates Johnson and Solon's analysis, using more recent data from the May and June 1983 Current Population Surveys, which permit her to include additional variables (e.g., firm size) in her estimated wage equations. Like Johnson and Solon, Sorensen concludes that a comparable worth policy would reduce the overall wage gap by at most one-fifth. Quite strikingly, however, the potential effect of such a policy is seen to vary widely across sectors of the economy. While she estimates that the policy might reduce the female-male earnings gap by about one-third in the public sector and by one-quarter in the nonmanufacturing private sector (defined by her to include all industries except for manufacturing and the public sector), it would reduce the gap in manufacturing by at most only 6 percent.

Of course, none of these authors' concepts of comparable worth really corresponds to the definition that proponents expound, namely, equal wages within a firm for jobs of equal value. The authors control for interindustry wage differentials and (in Sorensen's case) for wage differentials because of firm size, but these are incomplete controls for firm-specific wage differentials. Other studies suggest that the magnitude of the coefficient of the variable percentage female (that is, the percentage of workers in an occupation who are female) is sensitive to the variables that are included in the wage equation, so that more controls reduce the magnitude (see, for example, Filer 1987). Moreover, as Johnson and Solon and Sorensen note, their estimated comparable worth effects would be diminished if coverage of comparable worth was incomplete. Formal job evaluations tend to be conducted only by large firms, and Johnson and Solon conjecture that only 40 percent of workers, namely those employed by the government and by large private firms, would be affected. Assuming that the magnitude of the female-male wage gap does not depend on whether an individual employer would be covered by comparable worth, they further estimate that the overall effect would be to reduce the wage gap by only 1.4 to 3.2 percent, far less than one-tenth of the overall gap.

Sorensen's (1987b) results are relevant to this point. While coverage of workers under comparable worth might be large in manufacturing, where many workers are employed in large establishments (U.S. Bureau of the Census 1985a) her evidence cited above suggests that comparable worth would have a small effect in this sector. In contrast, in the nonmanufacturing private sector, where she estimated comparable worth to have the potential to reduce the wage gap by one-quarter, only a small fraction of the employees would likely be covered. If coverage was restricted to workers in firms with at least one hundred employees, for example, only about 49 percent in the service industry and 48 percent in retail trade would be covered (U.S. Bureau of the Census 1985b, table 5, and U.S. Bureau of the Census 1985c, table 5). If the minimum size for coverage was set at five hundred employees, these numbers would fall to about 29 percent and 38 percent respectively.

Of course, these crude calculations assume that females and males are distributed across firms of different sizes in the same manner and that all employees, not just those in occupations that are predominantly female, would be eligible for comparable worth wage adjustments. Smith (1988) made more refined calculations using the May 1979 Current Population Survey data, which have information on individuals' industry, occupation, and size of employer, to estimate the maximum percentage of women who might have their wages adjusted as a result of a comparable worth policy. He assumes that only females employed in jobs that are at least 60 percent female and are either nonteaching jobs in the public sector (since it is hard to envision other jobs "comparable" to teachers in education) or private-sector jobs in firms that have at least five hundred employees, would be eligible for such wage adjustments. Using these criteria, he concludes that only 23 percent of all female workers would likely be covered by a comparable worth policy and that they would tend to be higher-paid women. So, overall, the effects of comparable worth on women's wages might be even smaller than Johnson and Solon estimate.

Ex Post Studies. After a well-publicized strike over the issue, San Jose, California, was the first city in the United States to implement comparable worth for its employees via the collective bargaining process. Five wage adjustments to achieve comparable worth took place during the July 1981–July 1984 period. Two studies (Kahn 1987 and Killingsworth 1987a) provide estimates of what the effects of these adjustments were. Both these studies try to make inferences based on before and after comparisons, which require them to infer what would have happened in San Jose in the post-1981 period in the absence of the adjustments. As the discussion will indicate, this is not a simple task.

Shulamit Kahn focuses on the wage increases for those San Jose city jobs that were targeted to receive comparable worth increases and contrasts them to the wage increases in nontargeted city jobs. She finds that during the July 1980–July 1986 period the wage increases in targeted jobs averaged 74 percent. In contrast, the wage increases for other jobs in the city (*not* just those that had been part of an original pay equity survey) averaged about 50 percent during the period. Because a similar pattern of relative wage changes was not observed for jobs in other nearby local governments, she concludes that the observed difference in San Jose may have been due to the comparable worth efforts. I say "may" here because, although the other job wage scales in San Jose were roughly equal in 1980 to those in the surrounding areas, the wage scales in the jobs targeted to receive comparable worth increases were somewhat lower in San Jose. Hence some of the observed difference in wage increases may simply have been responses to market forces, although Kahn does note that in 1980 wages in San Jose in the targeted public-sector occupations (clerical) were higher than the wages in these occupations in the private sector.

Mark R. Killingsworth (1987a) focuses his analysis on the 170 full-time job classifications that were part of the original pay equity survey. He finds that between October 1981 (*after* the implementation of the first comparable worth wage adjustment) and July 1986, mean pay increased by 30.5 percent and 38.1 percent in the male-dominated and female-dominated jobs respectively, which, like Kahn's analysis, suggests that comparable worth may have had an effect (smaller in his case) on wages in female-dominated occupations.

To model more formally whether comparable worth adjustments affected wages in both the female-dominated and male-dominated occupations in the city, Killingsworth conducted both cross-section and longitudinal econometric analyses. As he notes, the longitudinal analyses, in particular his fixed and random effects models, are preferable.

In both cases, Killingsworth used salary data by occupation for eight points in time (July 1980, October 1980, October 1981, January 1983, August 1983, March 1984, April 1985, and July 1986); the first two dates preceded the implementation of comparable worth, while the latter six were during and after implementation. The logarithm of the salary in occupation i at time t is specified to be a linear function of a time trend term (the number of days between July 1980 and the date), a dummy variable that takes on the value of one once comparable worth is implemented (the last six dates) and zero otherwise, and an occupation-specific effect that is assumed to be either fixed or random. The models are estimated separately for the male-dominated, and female-dominated occupations, and in each case the coefficient of comparable worth is interpreted as indicating by how much, on average, comparable worth increased wages in these occupations.

Killingsworth found that, on average, comparable worth caused the wages of males to increase by about 9 percent more than would have been the case and the wages of females to rise by about 12 percent more. As such, he concludes that comparable worth in San Jose increased women's wages by about 3 percent relative to those of men during the period; this difference was statistically significant from zero in the fixed effects model but not in the random effects model. He thus finds much smaller effects for comparable worth than Kahn did.

Killingsworth's findings, however, raise two questions. First, why should comparable worth wage adjustments in female-dominated jobs cause wages to rise faster than would otherwise be the case in *male*-dominated jobs? Indeed, one fear of critics of comparable worth is that comparable worth wage increases would be financed by restricting wage increases in other public-sector jobs; one might thus expect comparable worth adjustments to reduce wage increases in male-dominated jobs.

This leads to the second question: why should one assume (as Killingsworth's model implicitly does) that in the absence of comparable worth adjustments, wages would have increased at a constant rate in San Jose during the July 1980–July 1986 period? In fact, average hourly earnings growth varied considerably for the economy as a whole during this period, falling from more than 9 percent in 1980 and 1981 to less than 4 percent in 1984, 1985, and 1986. The effects he attributes to comparable worth may reflect only underlying nonlinear trends in earnings growth in San Jose.

Killingsworth (1987b) uses essentially the same methodological approach to estimate the effects of three sets of comparable worth wage adjustments that were legislatively enacted for Minnesota state employees between 1983 and 1986 (these became effective in July 1983, July 1984, and July 1985). He analyzes data for a random sample of one thousand white male and one thousand white female employees who were present and active in state employment during the entire October 1981–April 1986 period and asks whether, after holding constant changes in personal characteristics and allowing for long-term pay trends, salary increases were larger for women than for men after the comparable worth wage adjustments. He concludes that the women's wages grew cumulatively by about 7 percent *more* and the men's wages by about 1.4 percent *less* than they would have in the absence of comparable worth. One must, however, again question his assumptions of constant trend growth rates in the absence of the comparable worth adjustments.

Peter F. Orazem and J. Peter Matilla (1987) used a different approach to estimate the impact of a comparable worth policy on the wage gap of Iowa state employees. Based on a job evaluation study conducted by Arthur Young and Associates, a pay equity program was proposed in 1984 for these employees. The proposal, which called for wage decreases for about 40 percent of the covered employees, was subject to considerable political debate, and eventually a "compromise" program was adopted in 1985 that moderated the wage increases "winners" received and eliminated all the proposed reductions.

Orazem and Matilla used data on a random sample of state employees and estimated wage equations for them using as explanatory variables individual characteristics, job evaluation point scores, and several other variables, including whether the employee was a woman. Three different wage outcomes were analyzed: the employee's actual wage scale as of December 1983 (prior to the comparable worth plan), the employee's wage scale as proposed under the Arthur Young plan, and the employee's wage scale after the implementation of the political compromise. Focusing on how the coefficient of the "female" variable changed with the wage outcome used enabled the authors to estimate the effects of the original comparable worth proposal and the compromise that was adopted on the male-female wage differential.

The precise estimates the authors obtained are somewhat sensitive to the explanatory variables they included in their equations. Some of their specifications included private-sector market wage rates for occupations, as measured by an annual wage survey conducted by the state—presumably proponents of comparable worth would prefer to see this variable excluded. Some specifications included the job evaluation point scores, while others did not. Nonetheless, all tended to suggest that the pay equity policy that was actually implemented reduced the unexplained (by the wage equations) wage gap by about one-quarter, whereas the gap would have been almost completely eliminated by the proposed policy.

In an absolute sense, their estimates suggest that the policy that was implemented increased the wage scale of the average female state employee in Iowa by about 1 to 4 percentage points relative to the wage scale of the average male. These numbers should be contrasted to the average 8 percentage point gain that they estimate would have been produced by the original Arthur Young pay equity proposal. Comparable worth policies implemented through the political process do not necessarily lead to "comparable worth." Indeed, using analyses similar to those of Orazem and Matilla (1987), Killingsworth (1987b) reaches this same conclusion.

Effect on Employment Levels

As with studies of the effect of comparable worth on earnings, studies of the effect of comparable worth on levels of employment have been both ex ante and ex post in nature. Among those who have conducted studies in the former category are Ehrenberg and Smith (1987a, 1987b) and Ehrenberg, Smith, and Stratka (1986), who simulated the effect of imposing comparable worth on the employment levels of women in the state and local sectors, and Aldrich and Buchele (1986), who performed similar simulations using economy-wide private-sector data. Included in the latter category are analyses by Robert G. Gregory and Ronald C. Duncan (1981) of how comparable worth–type wage adjustments influenced female employment in Australia and by Kahn (1987) and Killingsworth (1987a, 1987b) of how comparable worth wage adjustments in San Jose and Minnesota, respectively, affected municipal and state employment levels in these jurisdictions.

Comparable worth wage adjustments (CWWA) would tend to increase the wages of female employees relative to those of males within any major occupational group (e.g., clerical) in that females are more likely to be employed in female-dominated detailed occupational groups (e.g., secretaries) that would receive CWWA increases. Similarly, CWWAs would tend to increase the average wage costs in those major occupational groups that contain many female-dominated occupations (e.g., clerical) relative to those major occupational groups (e.g., blue-collar workers) that contain fewer female-dominated occupations. As such, one might expect to observe decreases in the employment of women, both because of male-female employment substitution away from female-dominated detailed occupational groups within major occupational groups and because of substitution away from female-dominated major occupational groups. To the extent that CWWA increases for female-dominated groups are not "paid for" by smaller wage increases for male-dominated groups, average wages would rise, which would further depress employment levels for both men and women.

Ex Ante Studies. Ehrenberg and Smith (1987a, 1987b) used data from the 1980 Census of Population grouped by state (for state employees) and SMSA (for local government employees) to simulate the likely effect on female employment rates of a 20 percent wage increase for all female employees in these sectors. Their simulations are based on estimates of within-occupation male-female substitution elasticities obtained from a constant elasticity of substitution production function specification and on estimates of across-occupation substitution elasticities obtained from a translog cost share specification. Because the estimated elasticities they obtained were quite small, they concluded that a 20 percent increase for all female employees in the sector would reduce female employment levels by only 2 to 3 percent.

Aldrich and Buchele (1986) applied Ehrenberg and Smith's approach to private-sector data, using three-digit industries rather than geographic areas as units of analyses. They obtained very similar employment effects, from which they predicted that private-sector comparable worth wage increases in the range of 10 to 15 percent would reduce female employment levels by about 3 percent in that sector.

Although the loss of female employees in each of these studies seems small and should allay critics' fears that comparable worth wage increases in the United States would lead to large losses of female employees, it should be emphasized that these estimates are based on cross-section demand elasticities that use broad occupational groups (four in all) and that do not control for area-specific (in the case of Ehrenberg and Smith) or industry-specific (in the case of Aldrich and Buchele) variables that might influence either male-female employment ratios within occupations or the occupational distribution of employment. Ehrenberg, Smith, and Stratka (1986) used longitudinal data on local government employment and wages from the Equal Employment Opportunity Commission's EEO-4 data to try to control for such omitted area-specific variables. They also used a larger number of occupational categories (eight). These modifications did not fundamentally alter any of the conclusions, however.

Ex Post Studies. All the authors acknowledge that serious data problems limit the usefulness of the above studies for public policy simulations and that the simulations are often based on statistically imprecise estimates of parameters. As such, it is useful to turn to the ex post studies. Gregory and Duncan's (1981) time series study of the Australian employment experience after the institution of comparable worth–type wage adjustments found that relative (by sex) employment demand elasticities with respect to relative (by sex) wages were sufficiently small and that the substantial relative wage increases for women that occurred between 1975 and 1978 in Australia reduced employment growth for women by only about 1.5 percentage points a year. The estimated slowdown in employment growth was smallest in the public (close to zero) and service sectors and largest in manufacturing. Of course, whether 1.5 percentage points per year is a small effect should be judged in the context of an overall female employment growth rate of 3 percentage points per year more than the male growth rate during the period. Viewed in this context, the Australian policy reduced the employment growth rate advantage of females vis-à-vis males by one-third (1.5/[3.0 + 1.5]). As noted above, employment of males is also likely to be affected by comparable worth policies; Gregory and Duncan did not analyze this effect.

In later work, Robert G. Gregory, R. Anstie, A. Daly, and V. Ho (1987) present analyses of the Australian data that cover the period from 1966 to 1984. Although they conduct no formal econometric analyses in their paper, they note that women increased their share of hours worked in Australia during the period and that the growth rate of this group of women was dominated by a trend in which no sharp slowdown occurred after the large (in the range of 20 percent) comparable worth–type wage adjustments were implemented. From this they conclude that any effects of the policy on the relative employment of women must have been very small, although they note that they did not analyze the effects of the policy on total employment. In fact, Ehrenberg and Smith (1987a, 1987b) found in their simulations that the potential adverse effect of a comparable worth policy on employment of women in the United States would be primarily through its effect on total employment.

The two studies of the San Jose experience reach conflicting conclusions. Kahn (1987) finds that municipal employment grew more rapidly during the 1981–86 period in the public sector of San Jose than in other neighboring cities, that employment in the municipal jobs targeted for CWWA in San Jose grew more rapidly than municipal employment in nontargeted jobs, and that the percentage of female workers in these targeted jobs actually increased. From this evidence Kahn concludes that comparable worth had no adverse effects on employment, that higher wages in the targeted jobs induced more females to apply, and that affirmative action, or an increase in the labor supply of women in general, led to the increases in the employment of women.

It is hard to evaluate the validity of Kahn's findings because they are all based on simple comparisons of trend increases in employment across occupations in San Jose and/or across local governments in the San Jose area. Put another way, implicitly, she is assuming that, in the absence of comparable worth, municipal employment would have grown at the same rate for all occupations in San Jose and that this rate would have equaled the growth rate of municipal employment in neighboring cities. As such, she does not allow for the possibility that conditions other than comparable worth influence employment growth and labor supply across occupations and areas.

Killingsworth (1987a) estimates a fixed effects model using data for six points in time and the 170 full-time job classifications that were part of the original San Jose job evaluation study. The logarithm of employment in an occupation at each time is specified to be a function only of the logarithm of the occupational wage at that time, a time trend term to control for general growth in employment, and occupation-specific dummy variables. Separate equations are estimated for male- and female-dominated jobs, and he concludes that negative wage elasticities of demand, in the range of minus one, exist for both the male- and female-dominated occupations. Killingsworth attributes the increases in employment that Kahn observes to his time trend term (which is about 9 percent per year for both male- and female-dominated jobs). Given his estimate that the CWWA increased males' wages by about 9 percent and females' wages by about 12 percent, Killingsworth concludes that these wage adjustments actually "cost" San Jose's male municipal employees one year's employment growth and female municipal employees more than one year's growth.

Killingsworth (1987b) performs similar analyses for Minnesota using data for 876 male-dominated state jobs and 203 female-dominated state jobs over nineteen quarters during the October 1981–April 1986 period. He finds wage elasticities in the range of minus one for both males and females when starting wage scale data are used. Coupled with his estimated wage effects reported earlier, these data suggest that the comparable worth wage adjustments in Minnesota *decreased* female employment levels by about 7 percent and *increased* male employment levels by about 1.4 percent during the 1981–86 period. The estimated effect on women is equivalent to a loss of about one year's employment growth.

Of course, Killingsworth's results for both San Jose and Minnesota are contingent first on his estimated CWWA effects on the wages of males and females in these jurisdictions; as noted above, I believe there are problems with these estimates. Second, his employment equations do not permit interoccupational substitution (an occupation's wage influences its employment level only) and assume that omitted time-specific factors influence all occupations in a gender group identically and at a constant rate over time. Indeed, no thought is given to the possibility that comparable worth per se may have influenced the trend rate of growth of employment (one of Kahn's points) independent of its effects via wage rates. Although my own preference is for rigorous econometric modeling, such as Killingsworth's, the jury is still out on the effects of comparable worth on municipal employees in San Jose and on state employees in Minnesota.

General Equilibrium Considerations: Who Will Win and Who Will Lose

The studies discussed in the previous section ignore the partial coverage aspect of any comparable worth policy that is likely to be implemented in the United States. If comparable worth has adverse effects on employment rates in the covered sector, displaced workers may seek jobs in the uncovered sector, resulting in downward pressure on wages there. Even if the number of jobs lost by female employees in the covered sector is low relative to the wage gains induced by comparable worth there, it is not obvious that women as a group would gain. Women in the low-paid uncovered sector might find, for example, that their wages are lowered even more by the "crowding" of displaced workers into that sector (see Smith 1988).

Alternatively, increased wages in the covered sector might induce some displaced women to remain "attached" to the covered sector in the hope of obtaining a higher-paying job in the future. Thus the policy might lead to "wait unemployment" among females. As is well known, in this case the increase in the number of females who are unemployed might exceed the number displaced because of the increase in covered-sector wages caused by the CWWA policy, and the direction that female wages in the uncovered sector would move would depend on demand elasticities in both sectors (see Ehrenberg and Smith 1988, chap. 12, for a more extended discussion of wait unemployment).

Of course, in addition to influencing the allocation of women employees between the covered and uncovered sectors, CWWA may also influence the labor force participation rates and occupational choice of women. Higher wages in some female-dominated occupations might induce more women to enter the labor force and increase the supply of women to occupations in which the adjustments took place (Kahn 1987). Higher wages in these occupations might increase their attractiveness to incumbents and new entrants and thus reduce the mobility of women into traditionally male-dominated occupations. Finally, higher wages in traditionally female-dominated occupations might increase the supply of males to these occupations, thereby reducing occupational segregation.

Empirical research related to these topics has been surprisingly slim. As noted above, Kahn (1987) found that CWWAs were associated with an increased representation by women in targeted occupations in San Jose. Perry C. Beider, B. Douglas Bernheim, Victor R. Fuchs, and John B. Shoven (1988) simulate in a computable general equilibrium model some of the effects of a policy (like comparable worth) that raises the wages of females. Although their simulations likely overstate the effects of comparable worth, because the policies they simulate eliminate all gender differences in earnings within major occupational groups, they are the only authors who analyze comparable worth empirically in a general equilibrium framework.

Beider et al. find that comparable worth would induce more married women to enter the labor force and that increased employment for these women would be at the expense of employment for males and single women. Despite the loss of employment to these groups, they would gain in a distributional sense because of their increased wages. In contrast, married couples would lose (increased employment of married women would be offset by decreased employment for some of their husbands), and single men as a group would be the big losers. Beider et al. also present estimates of efficiency and employment losses under a variety of assumptions about, for example, coverage of comparable worth (partial or total), the nature of utility functions for married couples, the elasticities of supply and substitution, and employer hiring rules (applicant fraction or historical fraction), and are careful to stress the sensitivity of their results to changes in assumptions. Nonetheless, to keep their model "computable," they are forced to limit it to only two occupational groups (skilled and unskilled). This restriction prevents them from addressing a number of the issues described above.

Conclusions

As this survey has shown, we know very little about what the true "general equilibrium" effects of comparable worth are likely to be. The research described above has concentrated heavily on estimating what the direct effects of comparable worth might be on the female-male wage gap and what the likely direct effects of comparable worth wage changes might be on the employment of women in the covered sector. Although the authors of the various studies might disagree, the evidence appears to be fairly consistent. The studies surveyed above suggest that one of the direct effects of comparable worth will be to reduce modestly the overall female-male wage gap and that this reduction would be achieved at the cost of only small losses of female employees.

What is missing, however, is much discussion of the true general equilibrium, or second-round effects, that comparable worth would be likely to induce. Would the altered wage structure affect the occupational choices of males and females in the covered sector and/or employers' hiring decisions? Would the changing wage structure in one sector of the economy lead to alterations in the wage structure in the rest of the economy? Would higher mandated wages in female-dominated jobs lead to higher implicit hiring standards, or would employers compensate by providing less on-the-job training? Would these higher wages reduce occupational mobility for women over the life cycle and their earnings growth rates? (See Hashimoto 1982 for evidence that minimum wages affect earnings growth rates.) Analyses of issues such as these should be on the agenda of comparable worth researchers.

DISCUSSION

JANICE FANNING MADDEN

Ronald Ehrenberg has prepared an extensive and useful review of recent studies, including many that are not yet published, that measure the effects of comparable worth policies. It is difficult to comment on a literature review; it is even more difficult to comment on a review of a literature that I have not had the opportunity to read. I am certainly not in a position to argue with his interpretations of these studies. Rather, I accept his description of the "state of the art" and explore some of the questions raised by these findings. My comments focus on two areas: the general difficulties surrounding empirical and theoretical research on comparable worth and the extent to which empirical work can guide the implementation of comparable worth policies.

The consensus of the literature Ehrenberg surveyed is that comparable worth wage setting reduces the gender wage gap from 10 to 25 percent and that disemployment effects are minimal, so that comparable worth wage setting increases the factor share of women workers. While these wage effects are lower than the 30 percent level indicated by some advocates, they are large relative to the historical record of change in the female-male wage gap, which has changed only about 15 percent (up and down between 36 and 41 percent over the last twenty-five years).

Ehrenberg's survey is not likely to satisfy the concerns of many economists about comparable worth policy. Many economists view the central issue not so much as the size of the wage and employment adjustments involved but as the efficiency of those adjustments. The efficiency of the estimated adjustments depends critically on why jobs that employ disproportionate percentages of women pay less than jobs employing men. If women's jobs pay less because they are discriminatorily "devalued"—that is, the level of employment in women's jobs is not allocated, and/or wages in women's jobs are not set efficiently—then the wage, employment, and distribution effects of requiring women's jobs to be paid the same as men's may be quite different than if women's jobs pay less because there are unobserved differences between men's and women's jobs in amenities or productivity.

The empirical analyses of the effects of comparable worth wage adjustments reviewed here cannot address these concerns. These studies compare the labor market outcomes when comparable worth policies set wages with outcomes when such policies are not used. There are two ways to do this: ex ante, which compares actual labor market outcomes in a situation in which comparable worth is not used to set wages with the outcomes expected (i.e., estimated) when comparable worth adjustments are made; and ex post, which compares the actual labor market outcomes in situations in which comparable worth is used to set wages with those expected (i.e., estimated) when comparable worth is not used. Either procedure inevitably encounters the same difficulties that complicate empirical estimates of the magnitude of labor market discrimination or, more analogous to the issue here, of the effects of equal opportunity laws and affirmative action. Do differences between the projected labor market outcomes and the actual outcomes represent the "desirable" effects of the comparable worth policy (i.e., elimination of discriminatory or inefficient differences), or are they an artifact of the estimation of the model (i.e., measurement errors)? This basic question can be raised with respect to all empirical studies of policies to combat discrimination. The question is whether the initial differences correlated with gender are due to discriminatory treatment of equals or to unobserved differentials in productivity that are correlated with gender. In comparable worth studies, the question is whether differences correlated with the female representation in a job are due to a discriminatory wage-setting procedure for women's jobs or to unobservable differences in job and/or worker characteristics that are correlated with female representation in a job.

These problems of interpreting the estimated percentage wage difference between women's jobs and men's jobs of equal ratings are complicated because no economist has developed an equilibrium labor market model that explains logically and consistently how female representation in a job affects wages and employment. The finding that "women's" jobs pay less than equivalently rated "men's" jobs becomes more persuasive evidence that "women's" jobs are paid less solely because women perform them, and not because of errors generated by a poor econometric model, if there is a theory that explains how a labor market generates such effects. Claudia Goldin, for example, outlines an intriguing starting point for a historical model to explain how female representation in jobs affects wages attached to the job (see pp. 83–89).

While a model of wage setting in jobs is critical to an understanding of the efficiency effects of a comparable worth wage policy, I do not hold out much hope that successful models will be forthcoming soon. For the last thirty years, economists have been trying to develop a model of discrimination in labor markets. No one has developed a model on which there is consensus. On the one hand, economists who believe that discrimination is impossible in competitive markets use the absence of a model of persistent discrimination as evidence that persistent discrimination cannot exist and that the conflicting empiricial results are a measurement error. On the other hand, virtually every empirical study in the last thirty years finds evidence of large wage differentials by gender, and these estimates have decreased surprisingly little as measurement error decreased (i.e., as our data and methods have become more sophisticated and more precise in measuring productivity).

After thirty years of research, we do not have a theory of discrimination, but we do have stronger empirical evidence that it exists. I fear that the same process and the same failures are likely to occur if we concentrate solely on efficiency in our analyses of comparable worth. We will develop theoretical models that demonstrate that the empirical results cannot occur while, at the same time, we are developing better data and methods that increase our confidence in the empirical findings. Therefore, although a theory that provides an equilibrium explanation of sex-based wage differentials in jobs is more likely to convince economists than better empirical work and is also necessary to the design of policy, I expect that policy makers will ultimately find that only the empirical work of the type surveyed by Ehrenberg is useful in their consideration of comparable worth strategies.

This leads to my second issue: whether this empirical methodology can also be used to guide the implementation of comparable worth policies. Ehrenberg has guided us through a series of studies that quantify the aggregate employment and wage effects of comparable worth policies. Implicit in each of these studies is a specification of the differences between the overall wage structure across jobs in the absence of comparable worth policies and the overall wage structure across jobs after the implementation of comparable worth. Can we use the models that indicate whether an overall wage structure is compatible with comparable worth to indicate where an individual job title should be placed in the wage structure?

Ehrenberg hints at a case in which such a problem arose when he discusses the Orazem and Matilla study of the Iowa State comparable worth policy, in which the comparability of jobs was determined not only by scientific methods but by a political compromise. How do political compromises or pragmatic outcomes of the determination of which jobs are comparable compare to the econometric studies? Are there obvious reasons why some jobs are more likely to be "politically" set? And, are wages in these jobs set differently for "political" reasons or because the econometric models (or the job evaluation points) are clearly "misestimating" their place in the wage hierarchy? Henry J. Aaron and Cameran M. Lougy (1986), using the Washington State data, demonstrate that equally plausible specifications of the relationship between job evaluation points and wages result in radically different salary rank orderings of some jobs. If this is generally so, it is not surprising that a political implementation of comparable worth might order some jobs differently.

Do "obviously" incorrect rankings of some jobs imply that the entire procedure is dubious? Can we place confidence in the wage and employment effects derived from job evaluation and econometric methods that force gender composition of a job to have no effect on wages when these same techniques incorrectly rank order the salaries of individual jobs? Can we place confidence in the estimated effect of gender composition on wages that these techniques yield? Especially in the absence of a theoretical model, we should accept only robust results; that is, we should accept only results that hold for all reasonable specifications of the wage equation. If all reasonable specifications of the regression of job evaluation scores on salary show, for example, that the percentage of females has a significant negative effect, we can more easily accept that discriminatory wage setting has occurred. This does not solve the problems at the remedy stage, however, because these techniques are not robust in determining which specific jobs pay too little or too much. Wages in specific jobs are ultimately "politically" set because our econometric and/or job evaluation models cannot uniquely rank jobs; we can verify only whether the procedure is neutral with respect to the gender composition of jobs.

In summary, Ehrenberg chooses not to analyze the efficiency effects of a comparable worth wage policy. In that an analysis of the efficiency effects is impossible without an explanation of the link between the gender composition of a job and its wage level and previous work indicates that such explanations are not easily forthcoming, Ehrenberg wisely takes on the "doable" task of measuring how neutralizing the correlation between gender composition of a job and its wage affects the wages and employment of women and the earnings distribution. This question is less interesting, but it does have an answer. The answer is that the wage effects for women are significant, and the disemployment effects appear relatively small. The empirical methodology used to reach these conclusions has also been proposed to implement comparable worth policies, that is, to define the wage rank ordering of individual jobs. This use of the econometric methodology is problematic because reasonable alternative specifications yield large differences in the wages for some jobs. For this reason, the "political" assignment of the wage rank ordering of jobs is expected to differ from the order defined by econometric models.

Pamela Stone Cain

As Ehrenberg notes, events have overtaken the debate on comparable worth. The days of heated, even vitriolic, discussion of the policy have receded somewhat, and we are beginning to see research on the subject that attempts to set aside zealotry, rhetoric, and partisanship in a sincere effort to enlighten rather than obfuscate. In fact, the research literature on comparable worth is not only growing, but burgeoning. In this paper, Ehrenberg performs a valuable service by critically reviewing a set of studies that address the central questions surrounding the effects of comparable worth—both intended and unintended. Ehrenberg organizes his review around two types of research: before and after comparisons of situations in which comparable worth has been implemented (ex post studies to use his distinction) and simulations of its implementation (ex ante studies). These studies differ also in their sources of data, assumptions, and modes of analysis. It is thus all the more remarkable, as revealed by Ehrenberg's review, to find that their results about the impact of comparable worth are quite consistent.

The studies' findings converge most strikingly in their estimates of the degree to which comparable worth closes the wage gap. Closure ranges from roughly one-tenth to one-fifth, dropping to 3 percent when restrictions on coverage are introduced. Ehrenberg notes that in actual implementation there is often a discrepancy between the wage adjustments proposed and those achieved. Nonetheless, case studies of actual implementations show meaningful improvements for state and municipal employees. Simulations also suggest that even under very limited implementation, comparable worth would result in some wage gains by women relative to men.

This section of the paper is especially good in pointing out the nature of the circumstances that limit coverage under comparable worth and in emphasizing that the policy redresses only *within*-firm wage differentials. These are subtle and not-so-subtle features of comparable worth practice that have often been overlooked or misunderstood in earlier policy debate.

Ehrenberg characterizes the approximately 10 to 20 percent reduction in the wage gap as "modest." I would like to counter Ehrenberg's "half-empty" appraisal with the "half-full" perspective that emerges when one examines the results in a larger context.

The wage gap has many sources, and comparable worth can remedy only one, at least directly. Thus, from the outset, there is a ceiling on the effectiveness of the policy. Controlling for occupational or job characteristics, we know from a voluminous literature that about one-third of the wage gap is due to differences between women and men's productivity as proxied by education, labor force experience, and so on. This portion of the gap cannot be touched by comparable worth.

Another one-third of the wage gap appears to be unexplained, encompassing a whole host of unmeasured or unmeasurable sources of earnings differences, among them firm and industry characteristics and illegal pay discrimination as defined by Title VII and the Equal Pay Act. Again, comparable worth cannot address these sources of wage differentials.

It is, then, only the final one-third of the wage gap that comparable worth can attempt to remedy—that portion due to the different nature of the occupations held by women and men. Moreover, some portion of these interoccupational differences are legitimate under comparable worth and would be preserved. The policy would never result, for example, in adjusting a secretary's salary to equal that of her boss. To the extent that men hold jobs that require greater skill, effort, and responsibility than the jobs held by women, occupational pay differentials by sex would continue to exist.

This leaves less than one-third of the wage gap that can be affected by adoption of comparable worth. Against this backdrop, closure on the order of 10 to 20 percent can be seen as quite large. Given the high degree of sex segregation and stratification in the labor force, moreover, these results suggest that the policy is, in fact, fulfilling close to its maximum potential.

Furthermore, Ehrenberg's review demonstrates conclusively that comparable worth has a positive impact on wage differentials. As an intervention per se, the fact that it has any measurable impact is notable. Results from research on the effects of affirmative action, for example, are much more ambiguous and inconclusive than the results Ehrenberg summarizes.

Although it is outside the purview of Ehrenberg's review, it should not be overlooked that since the emergence of comparable worth policies in the mid-1970s, there has been extraordinary movement in the female-male earnings ratio after decades of stasis. In the early days of the pay equity movement, advocates promoted comparable worth with buttons bearing the legend "59 cents," to reflect the prevailing .59 female-male earnings ratio of the period, which found women earning 59 cents to a man's dollar. Over the last few years, these buttons have become obsolete as women's earnings have advanced to the point that they now stand at approximately 67 percent of men's. Although there are many reasons for this progress, most notably changes in work patterns and occupational distribution of younger women, comparable worth probably played some role.

In terming the wage gains afforded by comparable worth "modest," Ehrenberg is undoubtedly influenced by the promises of its proponents, who have tended to promote the policy as a panacea to achieve pay equity. But these claims should be seen for the necessarily inflated political rhetoric that they are. By the yardsticks I have applied, I would argue that the gains made by comparable worth are robust and substantial, and, within its inherent limits, the policy appears to be successful in meeting its intended goal.

The remainder of Ehrenberg's paper is devoted to an examination of so-called second-round effects of comparable worth. Most of these have been raised by critics of the policy and can be characterized, although Ehrenberg does not do so, as unintended and adverse. These issues have received less attention in the research literature, but Ehrenberg's review demonstrates that the evidence on them is again fairly consistent from study to study. Best documented is the finding that comparable worth would appear to lead to small absolute losses in female employment. It is difficult to interpret these findings as an indictment of comparable worth because "employment loss" as used in these studies is ambiguous. Does it mean that women drop out of the labor force completely, suffer chronic or short-term unemployment, or simply change employers? Each of these outcomes has very different implications for the earnings potential of women, ranging from highly disruptive to negligible.

As to other second-round effects, the jury is still out, for there is as yet little research on them. With regard to the question of whether comparable worth would maintain or increase occupational segregation, Ehrenberg cites Kahn's study of San Jose, which found increased representation of women in occupations targeted for comparable worth adjustments. This is hardly surprising in the short run; one would expect that the first workers to respond to an improvement in an occupation's earnings would be those who have traditionally filled it. As evidence for the claim that comparable worth would reinforce segregation, this finding is suggestive but inconclusive, and a longer time frame is required for an adequate assessment of the effect of comparable worth on segregation.

Ehrenberg concludes that we know very little about these second-round effects. What we know, and with regard to female employment we are on firmer ground, suggests that employment losses for women will not be large. Thus, at this point in our knowledge, an evaluation of the indirect effects of comparable worth shows that they bear a small cost. This is a cost, moreover, that comparable worth advocates had anticipated and are on record as saying they were willing to incur, although others may not be.

The paper ends with a call for more research on second-round effects. Although I agree that this is an important research area, I hope the call is not preemptive of additional research on first-round effects. Ehrenberg's review convinces me that the latter is still a fruitful research area.

First, the evidence presented in this paper suggests that the direct effect of comparable worth on women's wages—although substantial for all the reasons I discussed—is not large in an absolute sense and is unlikely to result in major disruption. Evidence on female disemployment also suggests limited impact. On the basis of these results, it appears highly likely that second-round effects will be limited, insofar as they are, by definition, indirect and, by their very nature, likely to be attenuated. Hence, because we probably should not anticipate major upheaval in the areas of female employment, labor supply, and occupational mobility, these second-round effects are less important in the policy arena and the case for doing research on them is accordingly less compelling.

Second, one of the great contributions of this paper is its insight into the politics and logistics of actual comparable worth implementations. The difference between diagnosed remedies and actual adjustments is often large and predicated on purely political considerations. More research is needed to understand better the immediate circumstances surrounding the implementation of comparable worth in order to inform efforts to simulate and assess its impact.

Third, on a technical note, there are potential drawbacks to the methodology by which the impact of comparable worth adjustments has been assessed. Most of the studies Ehrenberg reviews, for example, follow the now-standard practice of estimating job worth using a set of white male-dominated jobs. These jobs are by no means representative of the full spectrum of jobs in a typical organization, and variance on important or valued (for the purposes of compensation) aspects of jobs is potentially restricted. In addition, it has been argued that jobs dominated by white males are overpaid relative to their true worth owing to employers' preferences for such workers and restrictions exercised by unions and other institutional arrangements. If this is the case, then the resulting job worth estimates are biased. To illustrate, in a study of the New York City work force, job worth was estimated and adjustments were calculated in several ways. The results differed from one method to the next, and certain categories of jobs, especially those performed by minority women, fared especially poorly under the standard model (Cain and Wieler 1988). The assumptions of prevailing comparable worth practice thus deserve additional scrutiny to discover whether changes are called for in the way implementation is conducted and simulated.

Finally, other topics need to be added to the research agenda Ehrenberg develops. Almost all critics of comparable worth assume, for example, that any pay raises granted under it are not accompanied by increases in productivity. A better understanding of the impact of comparable worth on productivity would illuminate the debate over a number of second-round effects, such as the impact on female employment, as well as help assess the inflationary impact of the policy.

I agree with Ehrenberg that enough research has been done to discern emerging patterns and draw preliminary conclusions about the probable outcomes of comparable worth. His review is invaluable in crystallizing the central themes and results of research to date. There are, however, substantive and methodological questions surrounding first-round effects that together constitute a full research agenda in their own right. I would hope that these will not be ignored in the rush to build a full-blown general equilibrium model, for to do so would not only shortchange important issues, but compromise the quality of the very research Ehrenberg calls for.

REFERENCES

Aaron, Henry J., and Cameran M. Lougy
  1986   *The Comparable Worth Controversy.* Washington, D.C.: Brookings Institution.

Agassi, Judith Buber
  1982   *Comparing the Work Attitudes of Women and Men.* Lexington, Mass.: Lexington Books.

Akerlof, George A.
  1982   "Labor Contracts as Partial Gift Exchange." *Quarterly Journal of Economics* 97 (November): 543–69.
  1984   "Psychological and Sociological Foundations of Economic Behavior: Gift Exchange and Efficiency-Wage Theory: Four Views." *American Economic Review* 74 (May): 79–83.

Akerlof, George A., and Janet L. Yellen
  1988   "Fairness and Unemployment." *American Economic Review* 78 (May): 44–49.

Aldrich, Mark, and Robert Buchele
  1986   *The Economics of Comparable Worth.* Boston, Mass.: Ballinger.

Ashenfelter, Orley, and Timothy Hannan
  1986   "Sex Discrimination and Product Market Competition: The Case of the Banking Industry." *Quarterly Journal of Economics* 101 (February): 149–73.

Barrett, Nancy
  1984   "Poverty, Welfare, and Comparable Worth." In *Equal Pay for UNequal Work*, ed. Phyllis Schlafly, 25–32. Washington, D.C.: Eagle Forum Education and Legal Defense Fund.

Bartholet, Elizabeth
  1982   "Application of Title VII to Jobs in High Places." *Harvard Law Review* 95 (March): 945–1027.

Becker, Gary S.
  1957   *The Economics of Discrimination.* Chicago: University of Chicago Press.
  1971   *The Economics of Discrimination.* 2nd ed. Chicago: University of Chicago Press.

Beider, Perry C., B. Douglas Bernheim, Victor R. Fuchs,
and John B. Shoven
    1988   "Comparable Worth in a General Equilibrium Model of the
            U.S. Economy." In *Research in Labor Economics*, 1–52. Green-
            wich, Conn.: JAI Press.

Beller, Andrea H.
    1979   "The Impact of Equal Employment Opportunity Laws on
            Male/Female Earnings Differential." In *Women in the Labor
            Market*, ed. C. Lloyd et al., 304–40. New York: Columbia Uni-
            versity Press.
    1984   "Trends in Occupational Segregation by Sex and Race, 1960–
            1981." In *Sex Segregation in the Workplace*, ed. Barbara F. Res-
            kin, 11–26. Washington, D.C.: National Academy Press.

Bergmann, Barbara R.
    1986   *The Economic Emergence of Women.* New York: Basic Books.

Bielby, William T., and James N. Baron
    1986   "Sex Segregation within Occupations." *American Economic Re-
            view* 76 (May): 43–47.

Blau, Francine D., and Lawrence Kahn
    1981   "Race and Sex Differences in Quits by Young Workers." *Indus-
            trial and Labor Relations Review* 34 (July): 563–77.

Bowles, Samuel
    1985   "The Production Process in a Competitive Economy: Walra-
            sian, Neo-Hobbesian, and Marxian Models." *American Economic
            Review* 75 (March): 16–36.

Bulow, Jeremy I., and Lawrence Summers
    1986   "A Theory of Dual Labor Markets with Application in Indus-
            trial Policy, Discrimination, and Keynesian Unemployment."
            Journal of Labor Economics 4 (July): 376–414.

Bureau of National Affairs
    1981   *The Comparable Worth Issue.* Washington, D.C.: Bureau of Na-
            tional Affairs.

Cain, Glen G.
    1986   "The Economic Analysis of Labor Market Discrimination: A
            Survey." In *Handbook of Labor Economics*, eds. Orley Ashenfelter
            and Richard Layard, 1:693–785. Amsterdam: North-Holland.

Cain, Pamela Stone, and Susan C. Wieler
    1988   "Pay Equity in New York City: Results from Alternative
            Models." Hunter College. Mimeo.

Corcoran, Mary, and Paul Courant
    1985   "Sex Role Socialization and Labor Market Outcomes." *Ameri-
            can Economic Review: Papers and Proceedings* 75 (March): 275–
            78.

Dalton, James A., and E. J. Ford
 1977 "Concentration and Labor Earnings in Manufacturing and Utilities." *Industrial and Labor Relations Review* 31 (October): 45–60.

Davies, Margery W.
 1982 *Women's Place Is at the Typewriter: Office Work and Office Workers, 1870–1930.* Philadelphia: Temple University Press.

Daymont, Thomas N., and Paul Andrisani
 1984 "Job Preferences, College Major, and the Gender Gap in Earnings." *Journal of Human Resources* 19 (Summer): 409–28.

Dickens, William T., and Lawrence Katz
 1987 "Interindustry Wage Differences and Industry Characteristics." In *Unemployment and the Structure of Labor Markets*, eds. Kevin Lang and Jonathan S. Leonard, 48–89. New York: Basil Blackwell.

Doeringer, Peter B., and Michael J. Piore
 1971 *Internal Labor Markets and Manpower Analysis.* Lexington, Mass.: Lexington Books.

Douglas, Paul
 1934 *The Theory of Wages.* New York: Sentry.

Dunlop, John T.
 1957 "The Task of Contemporary Wage Theory." In *New Concepts in Wage Determination*, eds. George W. Taylor and Frank C. Piersan, 127–39. New York: McGraw Hill.

Ehrenberg, Ronald G., and Robert S. Smith
 1987a "Comparable Worth in the Public Sector." In *Public Sector Payrolls*, ed. David A. Wise, 243–88. Chicago: University of Chicago Press.
 1987b "Comparable Worth Wage Adjustments and Female Employment in the State and Local Sector." *Journal of Labor Economics* 5 (April): 43–62.
 1988 *Modern Labor Economics.* 3rd ed. Glenview, Ill.: Scott, Foresman.

Ehrenberg, Ronald G., Robert S. Smith, and John W. Stratka
 1986 "Implementing Comparable Worth in the Public Sector: Some Analyses Using EEO-4 Data." Report submitted to the Equal Employment Opportunity Commission, Washington, D.C.

England, Paula, Marilyn Chassie, and Linda McCormack
 1982 "Skill Demands and Earnings in Female and Male Occupations." *Sociology and Social Research* 66 (2): 147–68.

England, Paula, and George Farkas
 1986 *Households, Employment and Gender: A Social, Economic and Demographic View.* New York: Aldine.

Fay, Charles H.
      1987   "Using the Strategic Planning Process to Develop a Compen-
               sation Strategy." *Topics in Total Compensation* 2(2): 117–28.
               "External Pay Relationships." In *Handbook of Human Resource
               Management,* ed. Luis Gomez-Mejia, vol. 3. Washington, D.C.:
               Bureau of National Affairs/American Society for Personnel
               Administration. In press.

Ferber, Marianne A., and Helen M. Lowry
      1976   "The Sex Differential in Earnings: A Reappraisal." *Industrial
               and Labor Relations Review* 29 (April): 377–87.

Ferber, Marianne, and Joe Spaeth
      1984   "Work Characteristics and the Male-Female Earnings Gap."
               American Economic Review 74 (2): 260–64.

Filer, Randall K.
      1985   "Male-Female Wage Differences: The Importance of Com-
               pensating Differentials." *Industrial and Labor Relations Review*
               38 (April): 426–37.
      1987   "Occupational Segregation, Compensating Differentials, and
               Comparable Worth." Draft of a paper presented at the Na-
               tional Academy of Science Authors' Workshop Panel on Pay
               Equity Research, September 14–15.

Fischel, Daniel R., and Edward P. Lazear
      1986   "Comparable Worth and Discrimination in Labor Markets."
               University of Chicago Law Review 53 (3): 891–918.

Fogel, Walter
      1984   *The Equal Pay Act: Implications for Comparable Worth.* New York:
               Praeger.

Gerstel, David
      1988   "Running the Company." *Fine Homebuilding* 47 (July/August):
               68–76.

Gintis, Herbert
      1976   "The Nature of Labor Exchange and the Theory of Capitalist
               Production." *Review of Radical Political Economics* 8 (Summer):
               36–54.

Goldin, Claudia
      1986   "Monitoring Costs and Occupational Segregation by Sex: A
               Historical Survey." *Journal of Labor Economics* 4 (January): 1–27.
      1988   "A Pollution Theory of Discrimination: Male and Female Dif-
               ferences in Occupation and Earnings." Unpublished manu-
               script.

Gregory, Robert G., R. Anstie, A. Daly, and V. Ho
      1987   "Women's Pay in Australia, Britain, and the United States:
               The Role of Laws, Regulations, and Human Capital." Draft of

a paper presented at the National Academy of Science Authors' Workshop Panel on Pay Equity Research, September 14–15.

Gregory, Robert G., and Ronald C. Duncan
    1981   "The Relevance of Segmented Labor Market Theories: The Australian Experience of the Achievement of Equal Pay for Women," *Journal of Post-Keynesian Economics* 3 (Spring): 403–28.

Grune, Joy Ann
    1984   "Equal Pay through Comparable Worth." In *Equal Pay for UNequal Work,* ed. Phyllis Schlafly, 3–10. Washington, D.C.: Eagle Forum Education and Legal Defense Fund.

Haessel, Walter, and John Palmer
    1978   "Market Power and Employment Discrimination." *Journal of Human Resources* 13 (Fall): 545–60.

Hashimoto, Masanori
    1982   "Minimum Wage Effects and Training on the Job." *American Economic Review* 82 (December): 1070–87.

Hodson, Randy, and Paula England
    1986   "Industrial Structure and Sex Differences in Earnings." *Industrial Relations* 5 (Winter): 16–32.

Jacobs, Jerry A.
    1985   "Trends in Sex Segregation in American Higher Education, 1948–1980," in *Women and Work: An Annual Review,* vol. 1, ed. Laurie Larwood, Ann H. Stromberg, and Barbara A. Gutek. Newbury Park, Calif.: Sage Publications.

Jaussad, Danielle P.
    1984   "Can Job Evaluation Systems Help Determine the Comparable Worth of Male and Female Occupations?" *Journal of Economic Issues* 18 (June): 473–82.

Johansen, Elaine
    1984   *Comparable Worth: The Myth and the Movement.* Boulder, Colo.: Westview.

Johnson, George, and Gary Solon
    1984   "Pay Differences between Women's and Men's Jobs: The Empirical Foundations of Comparable Worth Legislation." Working Paper No. 1472. Cambridge, Mass.: National Bureau of Economic Research.
    1986   "Estimates of the Direct Effects of Comparable Worth Policy." *American Economic Review* 76 (December): 1117–25.

Kahn, Shulamit
    1987   "Economic Implications of Public Sector Comparable Worth: A Case Study of San Jose." University of California, Irvine. Mimeo.

Kanter, Rosabeth Moss
     1977   *Men and Women of the Corporation.* New York: Basic Books.
Katz, Lawrence F.
     1986   "Efficiency Wage Theories: A Partial Evaluation." In *National Bureau of Economic Research Macroeconomics Annual,* ed. Stanley Fisher, 234–89. Cambridge, Mass.: MIT Press.
Kaufman, Roger T.
     1984   "On Wage Stickiness in Britain's Competitive Sector." *British Journal of Industrial Relations* 22 (March): 101–12.
Killingsworth, Mark R.
     1985a   "Economic Analysis of Comparable Worth and Its Conse-quences." In *Proceedings of the Thirty-Sixth Annual Meeting,* ed. Barbara Dennes. Madison, Wisc.: Industrial Relations Re-search Association.
     1985b   "The Economics of Comparable Worth: Analytical, Empirical, and Policy Questions." In *Comparable Worth: New Directions for Research,* ed. Heidi I. Hartmann, 86–115. Washington, D.C.: National Research Council.
     1987a   "Comparable Worth in San Jose." Rutgers University. Mimeo.
     1987b   "Comparable Worth in Minnesota." Rutgers University. Mimeo.
     1987c   "Heterogeneous Preferences, Compensating Wage Differen-tials, and Comparable Worth." *Quarterly Journal of Economics* 102: (November) 727–41.
Krueger, Alan B., and Lawrence H. Summers
     1986   "Efficiency Wages and the Wage Structure." Working Paper no. 1952. Cambridge, Mass.: National Bureau of Economic Research.
     1987   "Reflections on the Inter-Industry Wage Structure." In *Unem-ployment and the Structure of Labor Markets,* eds. Kevin Lang and Jonathan S. Leonard, 7–47. New York: Basil Blackwell.
Kwoka, John E., Jr.
     1983   "Monopoly, Plant and Union Effects on Worker Wages." *Indus-trial and Labor Relations Review* 36 (January): 251–57.
LaNoue, George R., and Barbara A. Lee
     1987   *Academics in Court: The Consequences of Academic Discrimination Litigation.* Ann Arbor: University of Michigan Press.
Leibenstein, Harvey
     1957   *Economic Backwardness and Economic Growth.* New York: Wiley.
Leonard, Jonathan S.
     1987   "Carrots and Sticks: Pay Supervision and Turnover." Working Paper no. 2176. Cambridge, Mass.: National Bureau of Eco-nomic Research.

Lindbeck, Assar, and Dennis J. Snower
  1986   "Wage Setting, Unemployment, and Insider-Outsider Rela-
          tions." *American Economic Review* 76 (May): 235–39.
  1988   Cooperation, Harassment, and Involuntary Unemployment:
          An Insiders-Outsiders Approach." *American Economic Review*
          78 (March): 167–88.

Madden, Janice Fanning
  1973   *The Economics of Sex Discrimination.* Lexington, Mass.: Lexing-
          ton Books.

Marini, Margaret Mooney, and Mary C. Brinton
  1984   "Sex Typing in Occupational Socialization." In *Sex Segregation
          in the Workplace,* ed. Barbara F. Reskin, 192–232. Washington
          D.C.: National Academy Press.

Marshall, Ray, and Beth Paulin
  1984   "The Employment and Earnings of Women: The Comparable
          Worth Debate." In *Comparable Worth: Issue for the 80's,* 1: 196–
          214. Washington, D.C.: U.S. Commission on Civil Rights.

McArthur, Leslie Zebrowitz
  1985   "Social Judgment Biases in Comparable Worth Analysis." In
          Comparable Worth: New Directions for Research, ed. Heidi I. Hart-
          mann, 53–70. Washington, D.C.: National Research Council.

Mecham, Robert C., and Ernest J. McCormick
  1969   *The Use in Job Evaluation of Job Elements and Job Dimensions Based
          on the Position Analysis Questionnaire.* Lafayette, Ind.: Purdue
          University, Occupational Research Center.

Medoff, James L.
  1987   "Comment." In *Public Sector Payrolls,* ed. David A. Wise, 288–
          89. Chicago: University of Chicago Press.

Megdal, Sharon Bernstein
  1986   "Comparable Worth: Some Issues for Consideration." *Contem-
          porary Policy Issues* 4 (June): 40–51.

Meitzen, Mark E.
  1986   "Differences in Male and Female Job-Quitting Behavior." *Jour-
          nal of Labor Economics* 4 (April): 151–67.

Michael, Robert, and Heidi Hartmann, eds.
          Pay Equity: Empirical Inquiries. Washington, D.C.: National
          Academy of Science. In press.

Milkovich, George
  1984   "The Emerging Debate." In *Comparable Worth: Issues and Alter-
          natives,* ed. E. Robert Livernash, 23–47. Washington, D.C.:
          Equal Employment Advisory Council.

Miller, Ann R., Donald J. Treiman, Pamela S. Cain, and Patricia A. Roos, eds.
      1980   *Work, Jobs, and Occupations: A Critical Review of the Dictionary of Occupational Titles.* Washington, D.C.: National Academy Press.

Nozick, Robert
      1974   *Anarchy, State, and Utopia.* Oxford: Basil Blackwell.

O'Neill, June
      1983   "The Determinants and Wage Effects of Occupational Segregation." Urban Institute Working Paper. Washington, D.C.: Urban Institute.
      1984   "The 'Comparable Worth' Trap." In *Equal Pay for UNequal Work,* ed. Phyllis Schlafly, 263–66. Washington, D.C.: Eagle Forum Education and Legal Defense Fund.

Orazem, Peter F., and J. Peter Matilla
      1987   "Comparable Worth and the Structure of Earnings: The Iowa Case." Draft of a paper presented at the National Academy of Science Authors' Workshop Panel on Pay Equity, September 14–15.

Parcel, Toby L., and Charles W. Mueller
      1983   *Ascription and Labor Markets: Race and Sex Differences in Earnings.* New York: Academic Press.

Raff, Daniel M. G.
      1988   "Wage Determination Theory and the Five Dollar Day at Ford." *Journal of Economic History* 48 (June): 387–99.

Raff, Daniel M. G., and Lawrence Summers
      1986   "Did Henry Ford Pay Efficiency Wages?" Working Paper no. 2101. Cambridge, Mass.: National Bureau of Economic Research.

Ragan, James F., and Sharon Smith
      1981   "The Impact of Differences in Turnover Rates on Male/Female Pay Differentials." *Journal of Human Resources* 16 (Summer): 343–65.

Ricardo-Campbell, Rita
      1985   *Women and Comparable Worth.* Hoover Monograph Series. Palo Alto, Calif.: Hoover Institute.

Risher, H. W., and Charles H. Fay
      1988   *Report on the 1987 Survey on Salary Management Practices.* Scottsdale, Ariz.: American Compensation Association.

Roback, Jennifer
      1986   "A Matter of Choice: A Critique of Comparable Worth by a Skeptical Feminist." New York: Twentieth Century Fund.

Schwab, Donald P.
    1984   "Job Evaluation and Pay Setting: Concepts and Practices." In *Comparable Worth: Issues and Alternatives*, ed. E. Robert Livernash, 49–77. Washington, D.C.: Equal Employment Advisory Council.
    1985   "Job Evaluation Research and Research Needs." In *Comparable Worth: New Directions for Research*, ed. Heidi I. Hartmann, 37–52. Washington, D.C.: National Research Council.

Shackett, Joyce R., and John M. Trapani
    1987   "Earnings Differentials and Market Structure." *Journal of Human Resources* 22 (Fall): 518–31.

Shapiro, Carl, and Joseph Stiglitz
    1984   "Equilibrium Unemployment as a Worker Discipline Device." *American Economic Review* 74 (May): 433–44.

Smith, Robert S.
    1988   "Comparable Worth: Limited Coverage and the Exacerbation of Inequality." *Industrial and Labor Relations Review* 41 (January): 227–39.

Snyder, David, and Paula M. Hudis
    1979   "The Sex Differential in Earnings: A Further Reappraisal." *Industrial and Labor Relations Review* 32 (April): 378–84.

Sorensen, Elaine
    1984   "Equal Pay for Comparable Worth: A Policy for Eliminating the Undervaluation of Women's Work." *Journal of Economic Issues* 18 (June): 465–72.
    1986   "Implementing Comparable Worth: A Survey of Recent Job Evaluation Studies." *American Economic Review Proceedings* 76 (May): 364–67.
    1987a   "Effect of Comparable Worth Policies on Earnings." *Industrial Relations* 26 (Fall): 227–39.
    1987b   "Measuring the Effect of Occupational Sex and Race Composition on the Earnings of Women and Minorities." Draft of a paper presented at the National Academy of Science Authors' Workshop Panel on Pay Equity, September 14–15.

Steinberg, Ronnie, and Lois Haignere
    1984   "Separate but Equivalent: Equal Pay for Work of Comparable Worth." In *Gender at Work: Perspectives on Occupational Segregation and Comparable Worth*, ed. Barbara Reskin, 13–26. Washington, D.C.: Women's Research and Education Institute of Congressional Concerns on Women's Issues.

Stiglitz, Joseph
    1986   "Theories of Wage Rigidity." In *Keynes' Economic Legacy*, ed. James Butkiewicz et al., 153–206. New York: Praeger.

Strober, Myra H.
1984   "Toward a General Theory of Occupational Sex Segregation: The Case of Public School Teaching." In *Sex Segregation in the Workplace,* ed. Barbara Reskin, 144–56. Washington, D.C.: National Academy Press.

Strober, Myra H., and Carolyn L. Arnold
1987   "The Dynamics of Occupational Segregation among Bank Tellers." In *Gender in the Workplace,* eds. Clare Brown and Joseph A. Pechman, 107–48. Washington, D.C.: Brookings Institution.

Thurow, Lester C.
1979   "A Theory of Groups: Which Age, Sex, Ethnic and Religious Groups Are Relevant?" In *Income Inequality,* ed. John C. Moroney, 169–82. Lexington, Mass.: Lexington Books.

Treiman, Donald J.
1979   *Job Evaluation: An Analytic Review.* Washington, D.C.: National Academy of Science.

Treiman, Donald J., and Heidi I. Hartmann, eds.
1981   *Women, Work and Wages: Equal Pay for Jobs of Equal Value.* Washington, D.C.: National Academy Press.

U.S. Bureau of the Census
1983   "Detailed Occupation and Years of School Completed by Age for the Civilian Labor Force by Sex, Race, and Spanish Origin: 1980." PC80–S1–8. Washington, D.C.: U.S. Government Printing Office.
1985a   *1982 Census of Manufacturing: Summary and Subject Statistics.* Washington, D.C.: Superintendent of Documents.
1985b   *1982 Census of Service Industries: Establishment and Firm Size.* SC82–I–1. Washington, D.C.: Superintendent of Documents.
1985c   *1982 Census of Retail Trade: Summary and Industry Statistics.* Washington, D.C.: Superintendent of Documents.
1986   "1970–1980 Census Comparability: Chart B." Unpublished.
1987a   *Money Income and Poverty Status of Families and Persons in the United States: 1986.* Current Population Reports, Series P-60, no. 157. Washington, D.C.: U.S. Government Printing Office.
1987b   *Male-Female Differences in Work Experience, Occupation, and Earnings: 1984.* Current Population Reports, Series P-70, no. 10. Washington, D.C.: U.S. Government Printing Office.

Viscusi, W. Kip
1980   "Sex Differences in Worker Quitting." *Review of Economics and Statistics* 62 (August): 388–98.

Waintroob, Andrea R.
1979–80 "The Developing Law of Equal Employment Opportunity at the White Collar and Professional Level." *William and Mary Law Review* 21: 45–119.

Wall Street Journal
    1985   Labor Letter. April 16, 1.

Wallace, Marc J., Jr., and Charles H. Fay
    1988   *Compensation: Theory and Practice.* 2d ed. Boston: Kent Publishing.

Weiss, Leonard
    1966   "Concentration and Labor Earnings." *American Economic Review* 56 (March): 96–117.

Whyte, William F.
    1955   *Money and Motivation: An Analysis of Incentives in Industry.* New York: Harper and Row.

Zanna, Mark P., Faye Crosby, and George Loewenstein
    1987   "Male Reference Groups and Discontent among Female Professionals." In *Women's Career Development,* ed. Barbara A. Gutek and Laurie Larwood, 28–41. Newbury Park, Calif.: Sage Publications.

CONTRIBUTORS

Mark Aldrich has taught at Smith College since 1968. He earned a Ph.D. in economics from the University of Texas, Austin. During 1979–80 and 1982–83 he worked as a senior economist at the Occupational Safety and Health Administration in Washington, D.C. He has also consulted for that agency. He has written on the economics of regulation and on women in the U.S. labor force. His most recent book, with Robert Buchele, is *The Economics of Comparable Worth*. He is currently writing a book on the history of workplace safety in the United States.

Rebecca M. Blank is an assistant professor of economics and public affairs at Princeton University, with a joint appointment in the Department of Economics and the Woodrow Wilson School. She has a Ph.D. in economics from the Massachusetts Institute of Technology. Blank has written several articles on the labor force behavior of women, particularly those who work part time. She has also published several articles focusing on the effects of government transfer programs on individual behavior and household well-being.

Robert Buchele has taught economics at Smith College since 1977. He holds a Ph.D. in economics from Harvard University. He has taught at the University of Massachusetts, Amherst and Boston, and worked as a CETA consultant evaluating job training and public-service employment programs in western Massachusetts. Buchele's publications include articles on supply-side economics, race and sex discrimination, and labor market segmentation. He is the author, with Mark Aldrich, of *The Economics of Comparable Worth*.

Pamela Stone Cain is an associate professor and chair of the Department of Sociology at Hunter College of the City University of New York. She received her Ph.D. from Johns Hopkins University. As a research associate at the National Academy of Sciences, she worked on the committee that issued one of the first major studies of comparable worth, commissioned by the Equal Employment Opportunity Commission. She is currently researching the role of women's job choices in maintaining job segregation. As a consultant, she has worked with corporations on equal employment issues and most recently was part of a team that conducted a pay equity study of the New York City work force.

Ronald G. Ehrenberg is the Irving M. Ives Professor of Industrial and Labor Relations and Economics at Cornell University and a research associate at the National Bureau of Economic Research. He received his Ph.D. from Northwestern University and is the author or coauthor of more than sixty articles and books in the areas of public-sector labor markets, wage determination in regulated industries, the evaluation of labor market programs and legislation, resource allocation issues in education, and compensation policies. He and Cornell colleague Robert S. Smith have published two empirical studies of the effects of comparable worth.

Charles H. Fay is an associate professor of industrial relations and human resources and associate director of the Institute of Management and Labor Relations at Rutgers University. His Ph.D., in human resources management, is from the University of Washington. He is the author or coauthor of several books, including *Compensation: Theory and Practice* and *The Compensation Sourcebook*. He is currently studying the impact of different pay practices on organizational success. Fay consults with many public- and private-sector organizations on compensation strategies and pay practices and has designed and installed a number of salary structures and sales compensation programs.

Judith M. Gerson teaches sociology and women's studies at Rutgers University. She received her Ph.D. from Cornell University. Her research focuses on the determinants and variability of gender relations. As part of that endeavor, she has recently completed a study of home-based office workers, entitled *At Home and in the Office*. She is working on a project on the distribution of resources in the household.

Claudia Goldin is a professor of economics at the University of Pennsylvania and recently served as editor of the *Journal of Economic History*. She received her Ph.D. in economics from the University of Chicago. She recently completed a year on a Guggenheim Fellowship in the Industrial Relations Section of Princeton University. Her current research interests focus on the evolution of the female labor force in America and the reasons for persistent differences in occupations and earnings by sex. Her book *Understanding the Gender Gap: An Economic History of American Women* is forthcoming.

M. Anne Hill is a visiting assistant professor in the Department of Economics and Finance and at the Center for the Study of Business and Government at Baruch College of the City University of New York. She received her Ph.D. in economics from Duke University. Her research interests include labor supply, wage determinants, gender differences in fertility and child care, and disability and vocational rehabilitation. *Disability and the Labor Market*, coedited with

Monroe Berkowitz, was awarded the 1987 Book Prize by the President's Committee on the Employment of the Handicapped. Her writing has been published in *Industrial and Labor Relations Review,* the *Journal of Human Resources, Rehabilitation Counselling Bulletin,* the *Review of Economics and Statistics,* and the *Southern Economic Journal.*

Marjorie Honig is a professor of economics at Hunter College and the Graduate School of the City University of New York. She received a Ph.D. in economics from Columbia University. She is the author of a number of articles on the impact of government programs on the labor market. Her studies of the Aid to Families with Dependent Children program were among the first to analyze its impact on labor supply and family structure. For the past several years her research has focused on retirement behavior, particularly the effect of Social Security on the labor supply of older workers.

Joyce P. Jacobsen is an assistant professor of economics at Rhodes College in Memphis, Tennessee. She received her Ph.D. in economics from Stanford University. She has done research on sex segregation, public and private and inter-industry pay and employment differences by sex and race, and work sharing.

Mark R. Killingsworth is a professor of economics at Rutgers University and a research economist at the National Bureau of Economic Research. He has M. Phil. and D. Phil. degrees from the University of Oxford, where he was a Rhodes Scholar. His research interests include employment discrimination, labor supply, and immigration. He has served as a consultant to parties involved in litigation under Title VII of the Civil Rights Act, including the U.S. Equal Employment Opportunity Commission, the U.S. Department of Labor, and the U.S. Department of Justice, and has given testimony on comparable worth to the Joint Economic Committee of the U.S. Congress.

Barbara A. Lee is an associate professor of industrial relations and human resources at Rutgers University's Institute of Management and Labor Relations, where she directs the graduate program in industrial relations and human resources. She holds a J.D. from Georgetown University Law School and a Ph.D. from Ohio State University. She is a coauthor of a book on the effects of discrimination lawsuits on the plaintiffs and defendant employers and has published numerous monographs and articles on employment discrimination, labor relations, and academic governance. She serves as an expert witness in employment discrimination lawsuits and is a frequent speaker on developments in employment law.

Janice Fanning Madden is a professor of regional science and director of women's studies at the University of Pennsylvania and codirector of the Temple-Penn Philadelphia Economic Monitoring Project. She received a Ph.D. in economics from Duke University. She has written more than thirty articles and books in the areas of discrimination in the labor market and spatial variation in urban labor markets. She has served as an expert witness in discrimination litigation and as a faculty member of the Judicial Center has taught federal judges economic techniques for assessing the existence of discrimination.

Elaine Sorensen is the research associate at the Urban Institute. She received her Ph.D. from the University of California, Berkeley. She has considerable expertise in the fields of women in the labor force, wage determination, discrimination theory, and occupational segregation. Her research has focused on comparable worth for several years. She is currently the principal investigator of a two-year study funded by the Sloan Foundation on the economics of a comparable worth policy. Sorensen is also an associate professor of economics at the University of Massachusetts, Amherst.

INDEX

realignment of wages within firms,
  effect of, 46
status of literature on, 37–41
effect on within-firm vs. across-firm
  wage differences, 85
empirical consequences of, 9, 90–116
  earnings gap effect, 91–100, 112–14
  employment levels effect, 100–4, 114
general equilibrium effects, 104–5
greatest potential for, 27, 28
industry wage premiums and, 23, 24–27
novelty of, 18–19, 34
outlook for the future of, 10
prototype policy, example of
  implementation of, 2–3
treatment in courts, 4, 10
Comparable worth wage adjustments
  (CWWA)
effect of, 93–94, 96–99
  on employment levels, 100–4
  on labor force participation rates
    and occupational choice of women,
    104–5
efficiency of, 107–8
Comparable worth wage gap (CWWG),
  computing, 92–93. *See also*
  Earnings gap, male-female
Compensating wage differentials, theory
  of, 21, 44. *See also* Industry wage
  differential
Control variables in empirical literature
  on occupational segregation, 63,
  65–66, 67, 68, 75, 76, 77–78
Courts, treatment of comparable worth
  in, 4, 10
Crowding, 47, 48
comparable worth legislation effect on,
  88
of displaced workers into uncovered
  sector, 104
inability of antidiscrimination laws to
  address, 54, 55–56
in lower and upper tails of wage
  distribution, 86, 88
model of labor market, 58, 59, 80–81
Current Population Surveys, studies
  based on
1978 data, 94
1979 data, 96
1980 data, 61, 62
1983 data, 95

on occupational segregation and wage
  gap, 63, 66–67

Daly, A., 102
Daymont, Thomas N., 22
Demand elasticities, employment, 101–2,
  103, 104
Dictionary of Occupational Titles (DOT), 60,
  69, 83
Direct-income transfer, 48
Discrimination, sex
alternatives addressing, 47–49
efficiency wage implications for, 28, 30
literature responding to, 38–41
litigation, 55–56
need for model of, 108–9
in neoclassical model, 42–43
"pollution" theory of, 8–9
preferences for
  male perception of women's effect on
    occupation's status, 86–88
  potential changes in employers', 52
theories on occupational segregation and
  male-female earnings gap, 58–60
transfer of income to victims of, 48
Disemployment effects. *See* Employment levels, effect of comparable
  worth on
Doeringer, Peter B., 33, 58
Duncan, Ronald C., 100, 101–2
Dunlop, John T., 19, 31, 34
Dynamics of comparable worth policy, 46

Earnings gap, male-female
comparable worth effect on, 91–100,
  112–14
  ex ante studies of, 91, 92–96
  ex post studies of, 91–92, 96–100
industry characteristics and, 24–25
occupational segregation and, 8
  discrimination theories on, 58–60
  empirical literature on, 60–68
percentage accounted for by differences in characteristics, 73–74
problems of interpreting estimated
  percentage, 108–9
reductions in, 9
Economic progress, shift of female distribution of human capital and, 88
Economics of comparable worth, 35–56
dynamics of, 46